HUE
hesi tate
HISPID
HUG
hydrophobia
HADDOCK
HOUSETRAIN
hachures
HONE
highjump
HADES
HAG
huff
HEXAPOD
HINDENBURG
hardy
haggle
HOIST
hoity-toity
hide
HARLEQUIN
hamlet
HUXLEY
H omb
HANDSTAND

haaf *n* In Shetland and Orkney, the deep or main sea. haar *n* A wet mist or fog; especially on the east coast of England and Scotland. haberdine *n* The name of a large sort of cod, especially used for salting. haberjet *n* A kind of cloth, as named in Magna Carta. habilable *a* Capable of being clothed. habochrome *n* Any of a genus of small South American rodents with large ears like a chinchilla. haboob *n* A violent Sudanese sandstorm. habromania *n* A kind of insanity which gives one the delusions of a cheerful or gay character. habroneme *a* Having the appearance of fine threads. habu *n* A venomous pit-viper of the Ryukyu Islands. hacendado *n* The owner of a hacienda. hacklet *n* A small species of sea-gull. hackmatack *n* The American Larch. hackneydom *n* A state of commonplaceness. hadbot *n* Compensation for an act of violence done to a priest. hæccity *n* The quality implied in the use of the word this; 'thisness.' haff *n* A shallow freshwater lagoon found at the mouth of a river. hafiz *n* A Muslim who knows the Koran by heart. haggaday *n* A kind of door-latch. haigspeak *n* Convoluted language of a type supposedly used by Alexander Haig. hakama *n* Loose trousers with many folds in the front, as worn in Japan. hakenkreuz *n* The Nazi swastika. halatinous *a* Salty. halecoid *a* Of or belonging to the herring family. half joe *n* A Portuguese gold coin. halichondroid *a* related to a group of sponges including the largest British sponge. haliwerfolk *n* Those who defended the body, relics, and territory of St Cuthbert. hallali *n* A bugle call. halok *n* In Scotland, a light thoughtless girl. hamate *a* Furnished with hooks. hambo *n* A Swedish folk dance in ¾ time. hamcases *n* trousers or breeches. hamesucken *n* In scotch law, the crime of assaulting a person in his own house. hammochrysos *n* A sparkling stone mentioned by the ancients. hanashika *n* A professional story-teller. hance *v* To excite with strong drink. hank *v* To fasten by a loop or noose. hapax *n* A word that has only been used once. haptodysphoria *n* The unpleasant sensation some people experience when touching cotton wool or running their nails down a blackboard. haras *n* An enclosure in which horses are kept for breeding. haratch *n* A poll-tax levied by the Turkish on their Christian subjects. hardometer *n* An instrument for measuring the hardness of metals. harengiform *a* Having the form of a herring. haruspication *v* Divination by inspection of the entrails of animals. hasenpfeffer *n* A highly seasoned rabbit stew. hastifoliate *a* Having spear-shaped leaves. haunk-haunk *n* The cry of a hyena. heanling *n* A base, abject or humble person. hecatarchy *n* Government by a hundred rulers. hecatomb *n* A public sacrifice of a hundred oxen. hecatophyllous *n* A plant with leaves each consisting of a hundred leaflets. hederiferous *a* Bearing or producing ivy. heian *a* Pertaining to a period in Japanese history from the late 8th to the late 12th century. hekistotherm *n* A plant that can grow in very cold environments. heldentenor *n* A powerful tenor voice suited to the singing of heroic roles in opera. helluo *n* A glutton. heloderm *n* A large and repulsive-looking venomous lizard. henbilt *n* A kind of fishing net. hendecasyllabic *a* Consisting of eleven syllables. hepe *n* A curved pruning-knife. herbelade *n* A kind of pork sausage-roll. hericide *v* The murder of a lord or master. hernet *n* A young heron. herio-comic *a* That which combines the heroic with the comic. hetman *n* A captain or military commander in Poland. hiaqua *n* An ornament or necklace composed of tooth-shells. hibernaculum *n* A place for hibernation; a den. hibschite *n* A member of the garnet family. hiccius doccius *n* A cant word for a juggler or one that plays fast and loose. hidrotic *a* Of or pertaining to sweat. hieratica *n* Papyrus of the finest quality. hierodule *n* A slave living in a temple, and dedicated to the service of a god. high-muck-a-muck *n* A self-important person. hijra *n* A eunuch, especially one who dresses as a woman. hill-woman *n* A woman who lives on a hill or a forewoman in a dust-yard. himbo *n* The male equivalent of a 'bimbo'. hinnible *a* Able to neigh or whinny. hippelaph *n* A large kind of deer. hipple *n* A little heap. hippolith *n* A stone found in the stomach or intestines of a horse. hircic *a* Of or pertaining to a goat. hircocervus *n* A mythological creature that is half goat, half stag. historiaster *n* A petty or contemptible historian. hobbledygee *n* A pace between a walk and a run. hobidy-booby *n* A scarecrow. hobohemia *n* A community of hoboes. hodiern *a* Relating to today; bang up to date. hoecake *n* Coarse bread, made of Indian meal, water and salt. hoer *n* One who hoes or uses a hoe. hoggerel *n* A young sheep of the second year. holour *n* A fornicator. holus-bolus *n* All in one gulp. Hom *n* The sacred plant of the ancient Persians. homerology *n* The study of Homer. hookem-snivey *n* A contrivance for undoing the bolt of a door from the outside. hop-o'-my-thumb *n* A dwarf or a pygmy. horcop *n* A bastard; also a term of abuse. hordeaceous *a* Related to or resembling barley. hornito *n* A low oven-shaped mound of volcanic origin. horriplilation *n* Goose bumps. horror-vacui *n* The dislike of leaving empty spaces, especially by artists. houyhnhnm *n* A horse with human characteristics. huckmuck *n* A strainer used in brewing. huggery *v* The action or practice of hugging. hugger-mugger *v* To keep something secret or concealed. huk *n* A guerrilla movement of the Philippines. humbuzz *n* A London name for the cockchafer beetle. humdurgeon *n* An imaginary illness. humhum *n* A coarse Indian cotton cloth. humicubation *v* Lying down on the ground, especially as a sign of penitence or humiliation. hummel *a* Hornless, usually referring to cattle or deer. hwyl *n* The fervour of emotion characteristic of gatherings of Welsh people. hydropot *n* A water-drinker; an abstainer from alcoholic drinks. hyke *n* A call to incite dogs to the chase. hylozoism *n* A theory that all matter is endowed with life. hyperparasite *n* An animal that is parasitic upon a parasite. hypobulia *n* Difficulty in making decisions. hypnagogic *a* Relating to the drowsy state just before you fall asleep. hypnopompic *a* Relating to the state between sleeping and waking. hyppish *a* Somewhat depressed or low-spirited.

Editor: John Lloyd
Art Director: David Costa

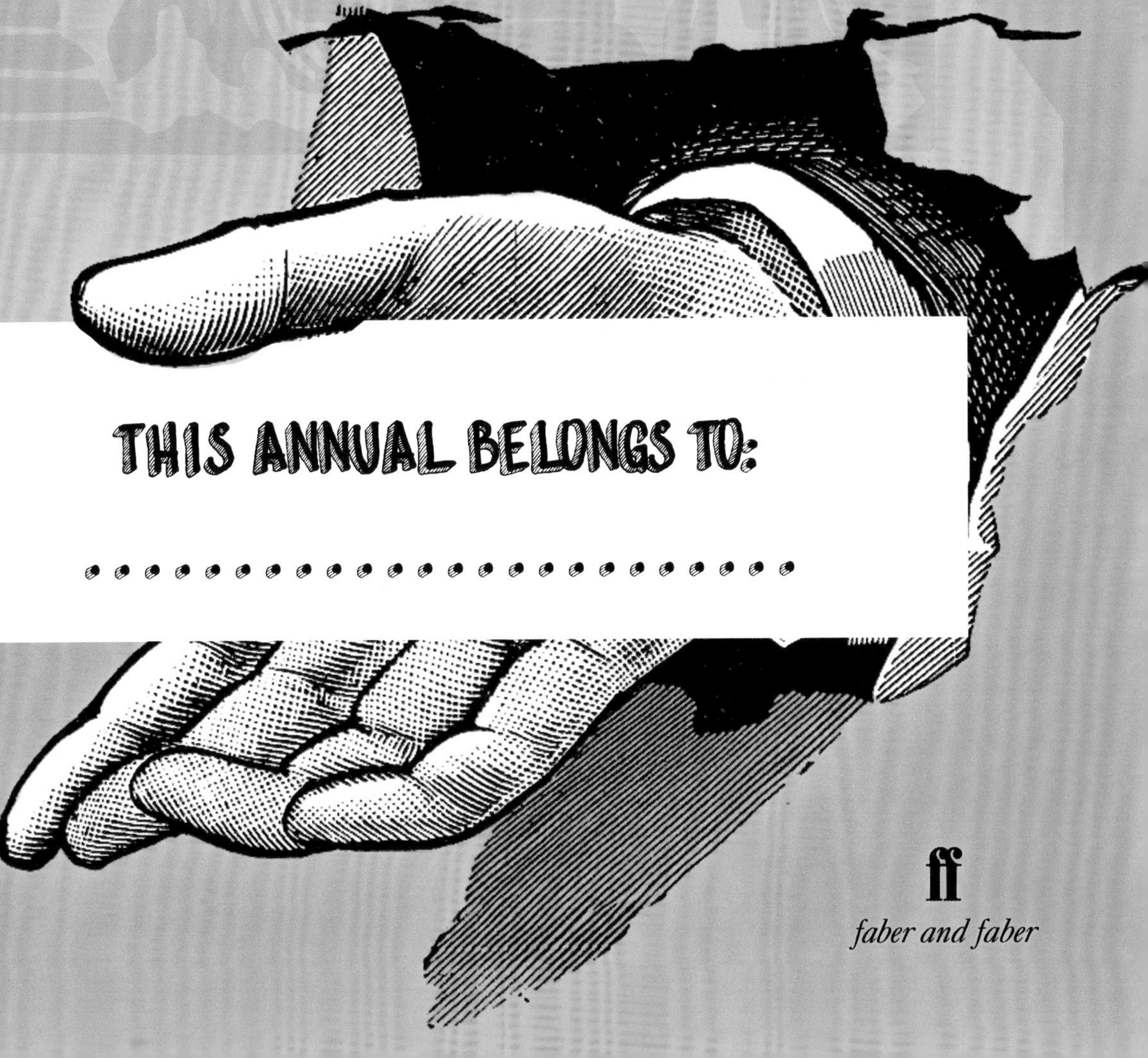

THIS ANNUAL BELONGS TO:

....

ff
faber and faber

WHAT THE H...?

INDEX OF CONTENTS

'Bloody Hippy!'

Newman

high jinks...

...and hilarity

Hello: A user's guide

Hello World

Hello, hallo, hullo. There are many different ways of saying hello in the world today. A Hong Kong hello (*Lei hao*) is often set aside in favour of the more important *Sik fan mei?* ('Have you eaten?'). In Taiwan, the Hakka Han people may greet each other in poetry and in Hindu cultures they break the ice with the word *Namaskar* – meaning 'I deny my ego and declare my faith.'

Hello Dalai

When greeting the Dalai Lama, make sure to bring a white scarf, or *khata*, for blessing. President Obama reportedly had a blessed scarf in his pocket during his inauguration ceremony in 2008. Another way to greet the Dalai Lama is to do what the mayor of Memphis did upon meeting His Holiness, and that is to offer him a fist bump, which apparently he will accept.

Hello Klingon

Should you ever get to meet a Klingon, be prepared for the fact that their language doesn't contain any means of cheery greeting whatsoever. A warrior race, the closest thing the Klingons have to hello is a curt *nuqneH*, or 'What do you want?' Most Klingons prefer to open conversations with a simple statement of business.

Hello Mam

When saying hello to the Queen, make sure you: ***(1)*** Never speak unless spoken to. ***(2)*** Call her 'Your Majesty' first, then 'Ma'am' (pronounced to rhyme with 'ham') every subsequent time. ***(3)*** Never turn your back on her. ***(4)*** If invited to eat do not start until she does. ***(5)*** If you drop food, pretend it never happened, and finally ***(6)*** never ask to go to the toilet. Just hold it in.

Hello Goodbye

Currently there are over 7,000 languages to say hello in. However, by the end of the century, according to National Geographic, more than half of these are expected to die out.

Hello Darkness

In Africa, the Dogon tribe of Mali start their greeting at some distance away from each other, so they can enquire about every member of the other person's family and their livestock, before eventually passing each other. The Zulu people will say, 'I am here' to which the customary reply is *Ngikhoma*, meaning 'I am validated' or 'I matter'. In Arabia, according to the explorer Wilfred Thesiger (1910-2003), firing a gun above someone's head was a sign of peace rather than aggression.

Hello Loneliness

In 1977, two spacecraft, Voyager 1 and 2, were launched on a journey into outer space. Each bore a gold-plated copper phonograph record containing, among other things: greetings in 55 human languages plus a burst of whale language; a 12 minute 'sound essay' including a kiss, a baby's cry and an EEG record of a young woman in love; 116 encoded pictures and 90 minutes of Earth's greatest hits, from Pygmy girls singing in Zaire to Chuck Berry's 'Johnny B. Good'. Carl Sagan, who chaired the selection committee, asked the Beatles if NASA could include 'Here Comes the Sun' on the record. The band said yes, but their record label said no.

Of the whole project Carl Sagan said, 'the greetings will be incomprehensible, but the intention is not. We thought it would be impolite not to say hello.'

By October 2011, the Voyagers were 17 billion and 14 billion kilometres away respectively – but still no answer yet. Fortunately, the shelf life of the golden records is projected to be 1 billion years.

Hello Kitty

Some animals, like humans, have their own ways of saying hello. Lobsters wave to each other, and dolphins sing in a unique tone, which effectively says, 'Hey! It's me, Gary!' Subconscious human-to-animal communication may exist as well. Research by biologist Rupert Sheldrake shows that cats appear to know when their owners are telephoning home and will jump up by the receiver before someone picks it up to say hello.

Hello Do You Do

The queen of American etiquette Emily Post (1872-1960) was suspicious of the word hello and said it should never be used between anyone except good friends. According to her, the correct greeting (to which no reply is required) is 'How do you do?' She was equally suspicious of handshakes, writing: 'A handshake often creates a feeling of liking or of irritation between two strangers. Who does not dislike a "boneless" hand extended as though it were a spray of sea-weed, or a miniature boiled pudding?'

Hello Sicko

When there are fears of a possible pandemic outbreak, saying hello can become rather difficult. 80% of all infectious diseases are spread by bodily contact such as kissing and handshaking. Rather than shaking hands, the World Health Organisation recommends 'elbow bumping' as an alternative.

Helloha

Aloha, the Hawaiian word for 'hello' has more than a hundred other meanings - including 'love', 'sweetheart', 'pity', 'alas' and 'goodbye'. The US state of Hawaii is written as HI.

Hello Heaveno

Leonso Canales Jr., a resident of Kleberg County, Texas, decided that he didn't like the first syllable of the word hello (hell-o), and came up with the alternative – Heaveno. He even managed to convince his county to officially recognise the word as its official greeting. They voted it in thus:

'NOW, THEREFORE, BE IT RESOLVED that Kleberg County adopts Mr. Leonso Canales Jr.'s universal greeting of "HeavenO" as the official greeting of Kleberg County and as a symbol of peace, friendship, and welcome.'

Hello Trolley

One place you can absolutely guarantee a hello is in Walmart stores in America. Employees (or 'associates' as they are known) are subject to a '10-foot Rule'. Whenever anyone gets that close, the associate is obliged to look the customer in the eye, say 'Hello' and ask if they can help.

Hello, I Presume?

Journalism's most famous hello – Stanley's 'Dr. Livingstone, I presume?' – probably never happened, according to leading Stanley biographer Tim Jeal. Stanley was known for taking journalistic liberties and the line was in question from the start. In all the letters Livingstone wrote about the meeting, he never once mentioned the famous quotation, and even Stanley's grandson, the late Denzil Stanley, openly questioned its veracity. While he later retracted this, his widow told Jeal that both Denzil and his father had their doubts.

Hello Doggy

Actor Dustin Hoffman noted that the way dogs greet each other may hold the secret to peace on Earth: 'If a lot of dogs are on the beach, the first thing they do is smell each other's ass. The information that's gotten somehow makes pacifists out of all of them. I've thought, if only we smelled each other's asses, there wouldn't be any war.'

ROGER LAW'S

HAIR TODAY GONE TOMORROW

A CONCISE GUIDE TO CHOOSING THE PERFECT HAIRSTYLE

WORDS BY EMMET O'SHEA

The **Mullet** first made its appearance in the 1960s and 70s on top of Tom Jones and David Bowie, before ruining its reputation by squatting on the pate of Phil Collins.

The highest thing to come out of the 1980s, the **Eraser Head** or **Hi-Top** combined short sides with a tower block of hair upstairs. This is the one for you if you enjoy a little break-dancing at the weekend, or if you're keen to meet more police.

The **Wafro**, sported in the early 70s by white American college kids, was a younger cousin of the Afro. Made famous by Bob Dylan and Art Garfunkel, it's perfect if you want to be laughed at by your parents when you come downstairs in the morning.

The **Beehive** or **B-52** (named after the B-52 Stratofortress bomber) hit the scene in the 50s and 60s with Audrey Hepburn and Brigitte Bardot. Scraggly pop princess Amy Winehouse has brought it back with her retro sound and style to match. Useful for stashing lipstick, car keys and cash - no handbag required.

The **Bowl Cut** was made fab by four young men from Liverpool and then later reinvented by another four from New York. Now when you walk into school, church or the lunatic asylum you can claim to be either one of the Beatles or the Ramones.

The spiky friend of Punks, the **Mohawk** requires enough hair gel to lubricate a tank. Created by Cossacks in the 1600s, it was a badge of strength, pride and leadership. It's now worn at concerts of the metal variety so your friends can spot and retrieve you from the mosh pit.

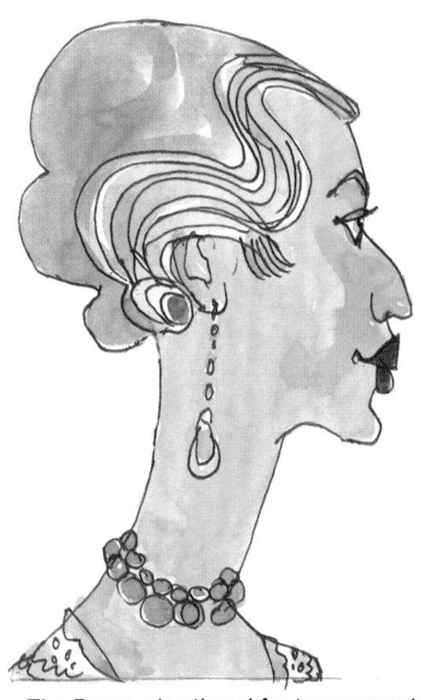

The **Perm**, shorthand for 'permanent wave', involves breaking the chemical bonds in your hair and winding it tightly round a 'perm rod', sometimes using extreme heat, so to achieve this look you need a scalp of stainless steel.

The perm hit the big time during 80s with stars such as Lionel Richie, Kylie Minogue and that crazy perm-wearing, God-bothering, goal-scorer Diego Maradona, who set the trend for footballers, football fans and, well, anyone who could say the word football.

To get that Donald Trump look, flop the sides or back of your hair over your shining dome. But beware the fatal midlife lure - the sports car. With your hairdo streaming out behind like Isadora Duncan's scarf, you could be strangled by your own **Comb-over**.

First it was big-framed librarian glasses, now comes **Trendy Comb-over** revival. Just grow your hair on top and allow it to fall trendily over your face. Being far too cool to use a hand to remove it from your eyes you will need to perfect the sideways head jerk.

Until recently wigs were associated with vain old men and magicians – the dead squirrel look. Then, in 2008, along came the latest bigwig, Lady Gaga, to show us all just what a **Wig** can do.

The **Duck's Arse** needs a BP oil slick and a comb. Gunk up your hair into a high quiff at the front, then slurp the sides into wings that join at the back like the rear end of a waterfowl. Don't go swimming: you'll be on the news for drowning gannets.

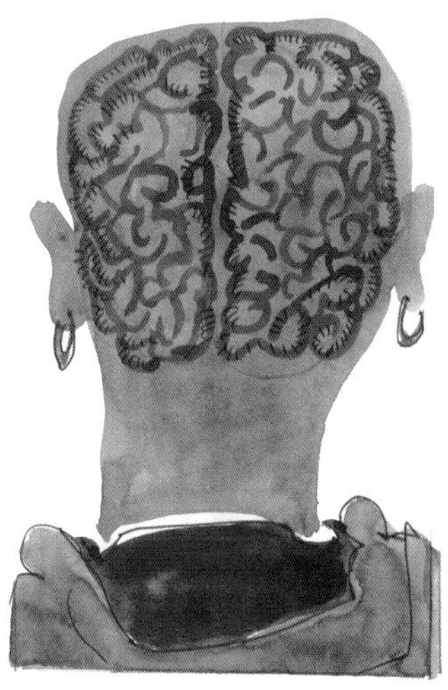

Want to let people know what's on your mind without opening your mouth? Why not shave it into the back of your head? It takes an extremely skilled barber to create **Shaved Sides**: intricate patterns or words engraved on your skull. This is where the fun begins.

The **Emo Tuft** was born in the first decade of the 21st century. It's a riot of swept bangs, layers of straightened hair and random streaks of colour, all piled on to create a wild confusion resembling one of the Cheshire cat's fur balls.

HEE! HEE!

'Run for it – it's the Pied Vuvuzela Player of Hamelin!'

'Oh no – it's the 4x4 Horsemen of the Apocalypse!'

'You come all the way to Glastonbury, then this has to happen!'

'It says: "Someone's invented the H-bomb!"'

Newman

Hard Questions - The H-Annual QI Quiz

With one person as quizmaster, you can play this at home. There are five rounds, each named after a degree course at Oxford University, with 8 questions in each. There are 2 points for a correct answer, but minus 2 for an answer that is 'obvious' but wrong. You can also give each player a joker that can be played before any one round. This doubles their score in that round. But anyone who gets a forfeit on the joker round scores double minus for that question. As John F. Kennedy said: 'Life is unfair, but sometimes it is unfair in your favour.' Nb: The keyword (or words) in every question, OR the answer, OR both, begins with 'H'. So, if the question doesn't have an 'H' word hidden in it somewhere, the answer must begin with an 'H'.

> It's no use trying to be clever; we are all clever here – just try to be kind, a little kind.
> *(F. J. Jackson, academic and don, 1855-1941)*

BIOLOGICAL SCIENCES

1. What unusual facial feature do horses share with the Mona Lisa?
2. Where did all the hedgehogs on Alderney come from?
3. What begins with H and has 32 brains?
4. What begins with H and can survive on nothing but wax? (HINT: It's a kind of bird.)
5. How many muscles are there in the fingers of each human hand?
6. Which mammal has the longest sperm?
7. Where are the smallest bone and the smallest muscles in the human body?
8. What does a trochilidist study? (HINT: It's another kind of bird.)

PHILOSOPHY, POLITICS & ECONOMICS

1. Which philosopher married a woman called Yellow Horse?
2. What's the original meaning of the word 'economics'?
3. Name the constituency represented by the only serving Labour MP with a butler?
4. Which famous philosopher was of peasant stock and was often mistaken on campus for a janitor or a heating engineer?
5. What kind of house was it that Sir Peter Viggers MP received £1,600 in expenses for?
6. Which country's unit of currency is the lempira?
7. Which successful 'economist' was the MP for Harwich, Essex in 1679 and from 1685-88?
8. James C. Humes was a presidential speechwriter for Eisenhower, Nixon, Ford, Reagan and George Bush Snr. The only speechwriter to have written for 5 US presidents, he has written 30 books and spoken in 40 countries. What is his most famous line?

CLASSICS

1. Which classical figure had a horse named after the same thing that the letter A is based on?
2. What's the immortal line of the haruspex Titus Vestricius Spurinna?
3. Who was President of the Olympic Games in 12 BC?
4. What begins with H and was the only thing left in Pandora's box after she opened it?
5. Name a famous Greek philosopher who was killed by parsley.
6. Which element is named after the Latin word for Copenhagen?
7. What's the Latin-derived name of the most magnetic element?
8. Name the hormone and neurotransmitter that is one of the few examples of a difference in scientific nomenclature between the US and Britain & Europe but both of whose names derive from the Latin and Greek for 'loins' respectively.

GEOGRAPHY

1. The horse the Duke of Wellington (who was Irish) rode at Waterloo (which is in modern Belgium) was named after which capital city?
2. How many cities are there in Holland?
3. Peter Kay and Vernon Kay both went to school in Horwich, home of Bolton Wanderers FC, who play there at the Reebok stadium. Which English county is Horwich in?
4. What geographical claim does the village of Haltwhistle make?
5. Where is the biggest mountain in the world?
6. What's the second largest island in the Caribbean and the 22nd largest in the world?
7. Where do they like hogweed soup and what do they call it?
8. Which is the only country in the world that has no hotels?

HISTORY OF ART, MATHEMATICS, HISTORY, ARCHAEOLOGY, LINGUISTICS, ENGINEERING, MODERN LANGUAGES, THEOLOGY, ENGLISH & MUSIC

1. HISTORY OF ART. What's the French for Hobby Horse or gee-gee?
2. MATHS & HISTORY. What number did the letter H signify in the Middle Ages?
3. ARCHAEOLOGY & LINGUISTICS. The word 'Holland' means the same in Dutch as 'Guatemala' means in Mayan-Toltec. What's the English for both places?
4. ENGINEERING. Answer *either* of the following:
   a. Which car was the first in the world to meet US pollution standards in 1972?
   b. What was the deathbed regret of Henry Royce?
5. MODERN LANGUAGES. Answer *either* of the following:
   a. What does Haagen Dazs mean in Danish?
   b. What language has no gender, no words for 'he' and 'she' or 'his' and 'hers'; no prepositions and no word for 'to have', no words for 'son' or 'daughter' but nine different words for a sibling and separate words for seven levels of ancestors and six levels of descendants?
6. THEOLOGY. The hymns *From Greenland's Icy Mountains, Brightest and Best of the Sons of the Morning* and *Holy, Holy, Holy, Lord God Almighty* were all written by Reginald Heber (1783-1826) who was a squishop and a squarson. What do those words mean?
7. ENGLISH. Spell hiccough correctly.
8. MUSIC. Franz Schubert was born in Himmelpfortgrund, now a suburb of Vienna, in 1797. He died in 1826 leaving his 8th Symphony Unfinished. In which key did he write it?

Tie-breaker on Vexillology*

Whose flag is this?

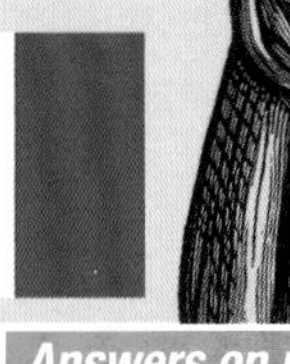

**The study of flags (not taught as a degree course at Oxford)*

Answers on p94

HOWDY
BY ROBERT THOMPSON
SO, YOU'RE DOC HOLIDAY
Sun Cream
Jackie Collins
REACH FOR THE SKY
Live Sport
Buffalo Bill
Electricity Bill
Gas Bill

PUT YOUR LEFT ARM IN
YOUR LEFT ARM OUT...
NICE 'N' SLOOOW
THE
HOKEY COKEY
CORRAL
I'M TIRED
OF RUNNIN'
MARTHA
THAT'S BECAUSE
YOU'RE OBESE,
JAKE
DRAW!
Arsenal 0
Chelsea 0

orsefeathers*
arcel Proust famously wrote in a cork-lined room. He was very sensitive.
And very buoyant.
I saw a headline once in Ireland. It said, 'cork man drowns'.
What disease can you get from decorating a Christmas tree?
Tinselitis!
The word 'Dyke' used to be slang for the vulva.
Why don't they just call it a family run-around with an excellent safety record?
How far away from a shark do you want to be if you cut yourself shaving?
I don't know. on top of a car park maybe?
How would you spot a Neanderthal if you saw one on a bus?
Is he the one looking at the wheels going 'What the Hell??'
The oldest trick in the book is pulling the head off a goose and then restoring it.
I can do the first half of that trick.

*An American expression meaning 'Talking nonsense'.

"good child-bearing hips." "snake" hips hippy hipster hips that pass in the night.

PEACE

HULA HOOP

In 1958, between 100 & 120 million hula hoops were sold in the USA.

IN THE 1990S THERE WAS A NATIONAL SCARE IN CHINA OVER THE CRAZE WHICH, IT WAS CLAIMED, HAD CAUSED A SPATE OF INTESTINAL INJURIES. AT LEAST 3 PEOPLE IN BEIJING WERE RUSHED TO HOSPITAL WITH TWISTED INSIDES.

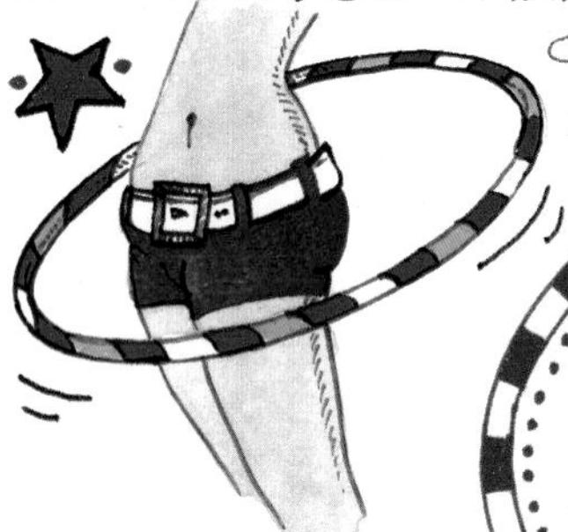

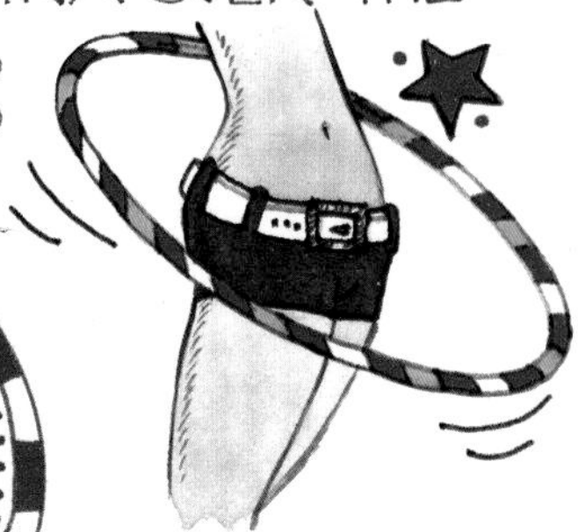

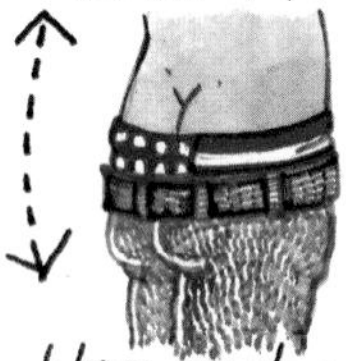

HIPS

In the suburb of Lynwood, Chicago, it's against the law for your trousers to be more than three inches below your hips, thus showing your pants.

FINE=$25

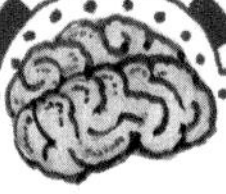

According to one recent study women with curvy hips appear to be more intelligent.

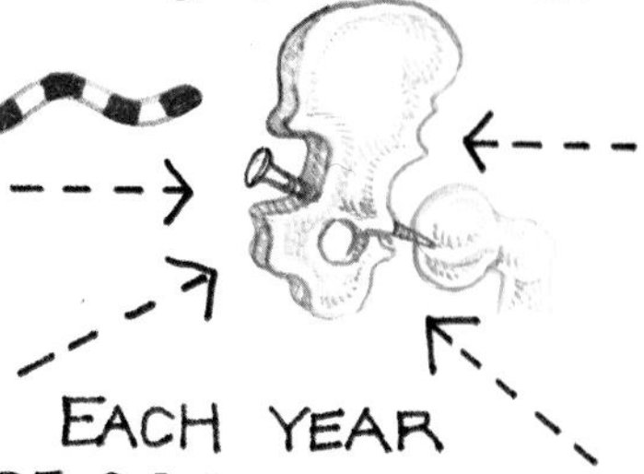

EACH YEAR 35,000 HIPS ARE REPLACED IN ENGLAND AND WALES ON THE N·H·S·

The first artificial joint was made out of ivory.

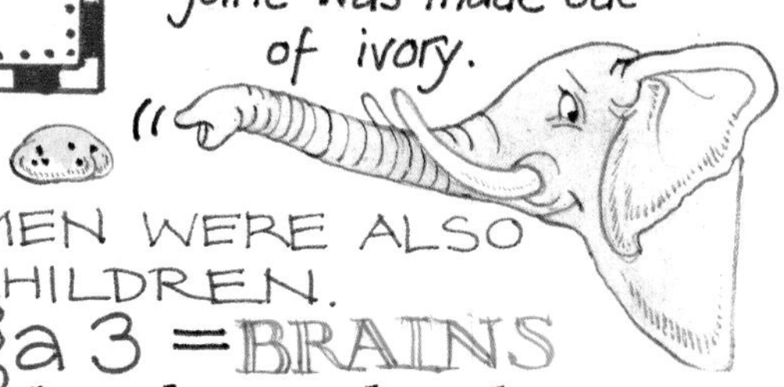

HOURGLASS-SHAPED WOMEN WERE ALSO FOUND TO PRODUCE BRIGHTER CHILDREN.

omega 3 = BRAINS

·hippie crack·

=laughing gas

·hipcat·

=cool person

·hipped·

=sad

·hip-chick·

=hotel prostitute

THE HISTORY OF HIRUDINEA*

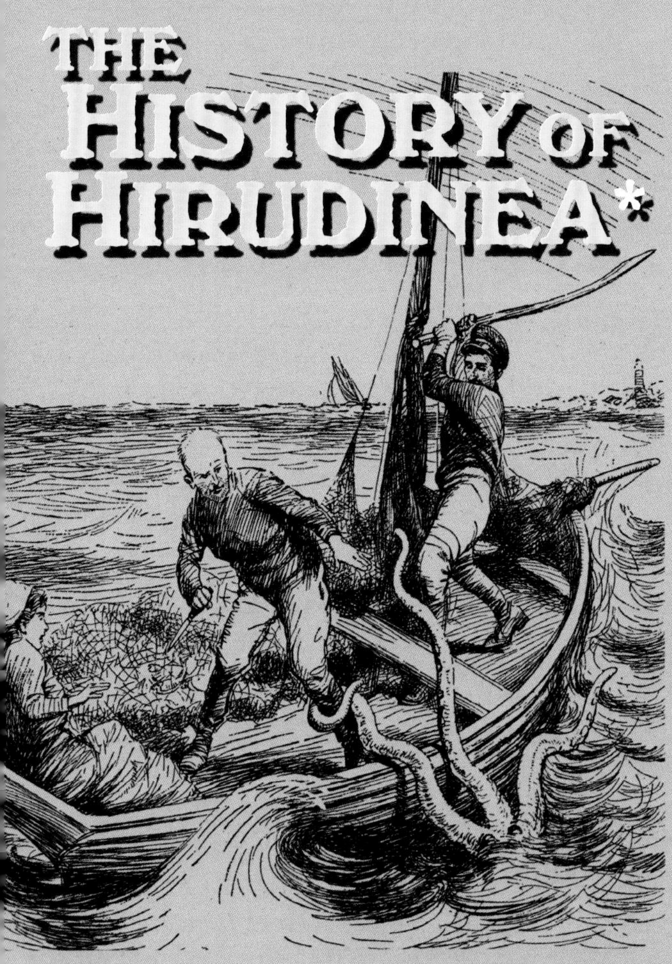

The largest known leech was 18 inches long.

Wales was once one of the major leech collecting areas of Europe. The Welsh would stand in lakes and pools and wait for leeches to attach to their legs.

Afterwards they plucked them off, put them in baskets and sold them.

Leeches can bite through a hippo's hide.

**more commonly known as leeches.*

By the 19th century, the use of leeches in medicine was so widespread that France imported 42 million in 1833 alone.

Today, leech surgery is back with a vengeance. British hospitals buy 12,000 to 15,000 leeches a year from Britain's only leech farm. Used for burns and plastic surgery, they cost £9.95 each.

Leeches are theoretically re-usable, but are killed by being dumped in a strong alcohol solution after use

Leeches are used for reattaching severed fingers.

An attached leech feeds for 30 minutes to an hour, swelling to five and ten times its original size. When full, it drops off.

Care must be taken when using leeches; once they have finishing sucking and let go, they have a tendency to 'wander off'.

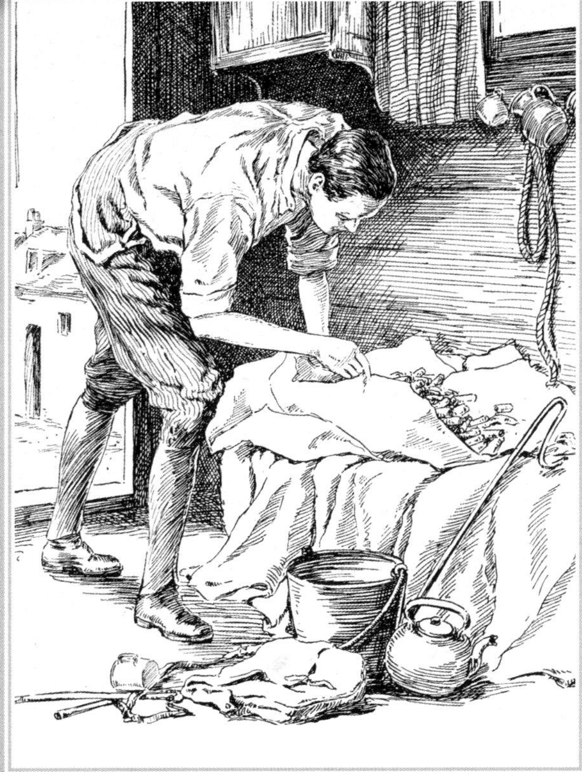

Nurses don't like rummaging in the bedclothes for bloated leeches.

Today, leeches have the same protected status as the white rhino.

Jo Brand's

Home Economy

How to halve your housework!

Always make sure you empty the ashtrays... into your husband's side of the bed.

Housework can kill you, if you do it right.

ERMA BOMBECK

PHOTOGRAPHY BY ANDY HOLLINGWORTH

Eat your tea actually on the table then get the cat to lick it clean.

Invest in a dark-coloured, patterned carpet; this will conceal any minor spills and match any major ones like spaghetti (or tapeworm).

Use a hairdryer to blow the dust off things. A dust-free cobweb or dust-mite is virtually invisible.

Use old pants as tea towels to save money.

Remove nasty smells by writing to your lawyer and divorcing your husband.

Keep a mop handy for when it's 'that time of the month.'

If troubled by silverfish, try placing whole cloves in closets and drawers. If you couldn't give a toss about them, take the morning off.

I have the Hoover on constantly so the neighbours can't hear my vibrator.

Remove the gunk from around the plughole with lady tweezers. I always like to pop it into a moussaka if we have some children I don't like coming for tea.

Decorate the house with plants that grow in the desert, then you don't have to water them. Big cacti on the windowsill also deter burglars.

Keep a large dead rat in the hall. This discourages visitors and cuts down on the mess.

Always wear an apron when you're cooking, then you can scrape stuff off the front of it to make a comforting broth.

A table, a chair, a bowl of fruit and a violin; what else does a man need to be happy?

ALBERT EINSTEIN

Our brains contain 100 billion cells called neurons, each of which can connect to about 7,000 others. These connections or *synapses* can be electrical or chemical. The electrical impulses are faster, enabling us to run, jump and poke buttons; the chemical connections are slower and control more complex behaviours and emotions. Happiness is a chemical process. Magic substances called neurotransmitters cross a tiny gap (or *synaptic cleft*) between the neurons. The next neuron detects and matches the flavour and the two cells click together, like a chemical padlock. Neurotransmitters include seratonin (which surges when you're exposed to danger, exertion, or intense fun), and endorphin (a painkiller 3 times more potent than morphine), which kicks in when you get hurt and explains the joy some folks feel during a Friday night punch-up.

BY TED DEWAN

THE HAZARDS OF

Happiness

KNOW THE DANGERS!
KNOW THE CAUSE!
KNOW WHAT TO DO!

If you observe a really happy man, you will find him building a boat, writing a symphony, educating his son, growing double dahlias in his garden, or looking for dinosaur eggs in the Gobi desert. He will not be searching for happiness as if it were a collar button that has rolled under a radiator. W. BERAN WOLFE

HAPPINESS IS FLEETING

Happiness is an evolutionary con- trick; an injection of feel-good brainjuice that rewards humans when they reproduce, form groups, eat meat and berries, and kill enemies.

But happiness is a transient feeling, and for a good reason: a species that spent all day just having sex, eating and hanging out with mates would be an easy target for predators.

HAPPINESS CAN KILL

In 1954, two Canadian neuroscientists pushed an electrode into a living rat's brain and accidentally discovered the brain's 'feel-good centre', the hypothalamus (which also regulates body temperature, thirst and hunger). When zapped with electricity, it produced intense pleasure and sexual arousal in the rat. The scientists then rigged up a device so the rat could press a lever that fired up the electrode. Once it worked out what the lever did, the rat spent the rest of its life maniacally whacking the lever, not stopping for food, drink, or sleep…

If I could drop dead right now, I'd be the happiest man alive!

SAMUEL GOLDWYN

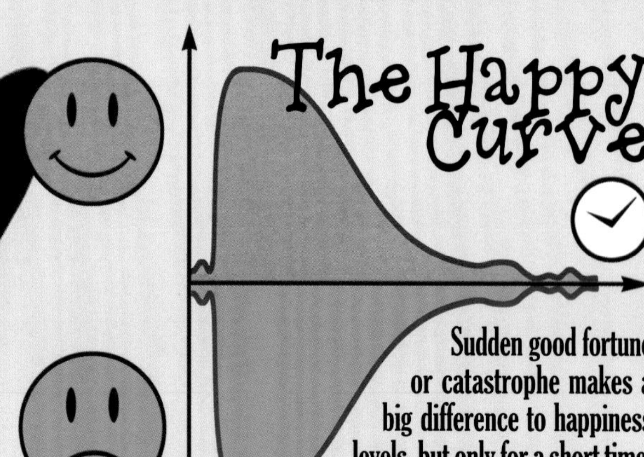

Sudden good fortune or catastrophe makes a big difference to happiness levels, but only for a short time. A UK study in 1978 analysed the happiness of recent lottery winners and victims of spinal-cord injuries. Their changes in status affected them immediately and profoundly, but within a year their happiness levels had returned to where they were before.

The Politics of Happiness

IN THE AMERICAN DECLARATION OF INDEPENDENCE, Thomas Jefferson wrote 'All men ... are endowed by their Creator with certain unalienable rights ... among these are life, liberty, and the pursuit of happiness.' By 'happiness', he meant physical health and psychological contentment. He never said that happiness itself was a right, just its pursuit, and he wasn't laying down an unalienable right to shop, party and consume more resources than any other nation. Surprisingly, high average incomes, long life expectancy and good public health do not make a nation happy: economic equality does. Nations with big gaps between rich and poor tend to be more miserable, with more futile searching for happiness in shopping malls. Jeremy Bentham, a British social reformer and contemporary of Jefferson's, founded the 18th century happiness movement called Utilitarianism, which defined happiness as 'the greatest good of the greatest number of people'. Bentham found personal happiness by keeping himself busy. He designed prisons, collected wild mice, slept with a pig, and had himself mummified. He still sits in a glass box in the hallway of University College, London.

FIVE WAYS TO GET HAPPY

1. Meditation

Can work wonders but involves a lot of boring practice.

2. Marriage

Married men live seven years longer than single men, married women four years longer than single women.*

3. Mood-altering drugs

These imitate and regulate the brain's natural happy hormones. But, as always, the 'Happy Curve' applies. A heavy drug-user's brain gradually changes so it can't function normally without being marinated in the drug. If the drug is suddenly withdrawn, the brain has to get used to working without it, which feels worse than drilling a hole in one's own head.

4. Trepanning

Drilling a hole in the head is an ancient form of healing believed to let evil spirits escape from sick people. Trepanners these days believe that the soft fontanelle on the top of babies' heads where the skull hasn't joined up yet, allows blood to flow better through the brain. Cutting a hole in a hard adult skull supposedly increases blood flow in the brain, re-creating infantile happiness. In 1970, 'open-minded' trepanning enthusiast Joey Mellen burnt out an electric drill after half-an-hour attempting to self trepan. He eventually succeeded and claimed the resulting hole gave him 'a permanent high'.

5. Flow

Probably the safest, cheapest, and most rewarding way to feel regularly happy is to be in a state of 'flow'. 'Flow' is the euphoria experienced when totally absorbed in something, usually just at the edge of your ability. This can come from playing an instrument, or racing a sports car, or even doing the ironing.

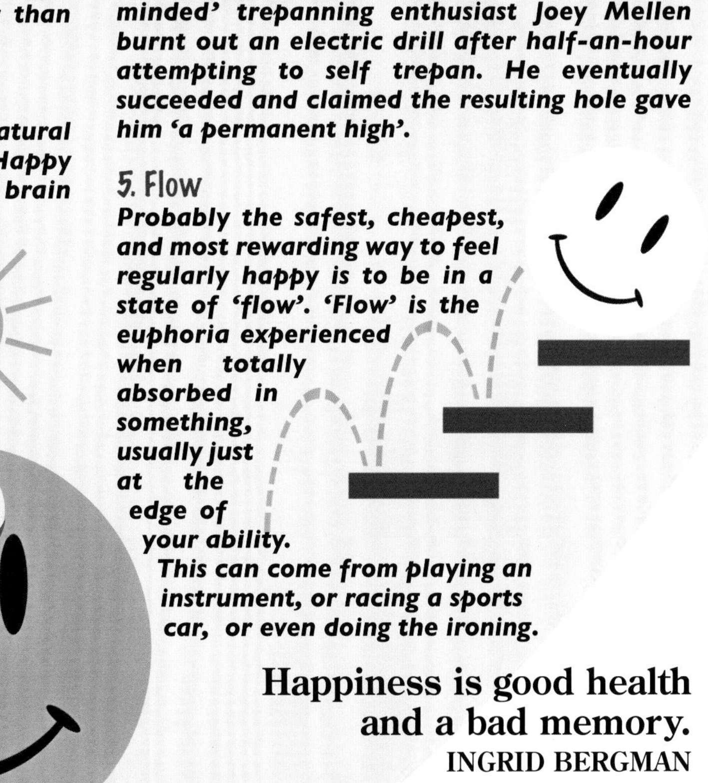

**Married men live longer than single men. But married men are a lot more willing to die.*
JOHNNY CARSON

Happiness is good health and a bad memory.
INGRID BERGMAN

Highwaymen

DON'T GO BY ROAD

NO NEW ROADS WERE BUILT IN ENGLAND FROM THE END OF THE ROMAN OCCUPATION TO THE INTRODUCTION OF GATED, PRIVATELY BUILT TOLL ROADS, KNOWN AS TURNPIKES, IN THE 1750S. THESE APART, ENGLISH ROADS WERE MUDDY, RUTTED AND BADLY SIGNPOSTED – OFFERING AN EASY OPPORTUNITY FOR THIEVES. FEW ORDINARY PEOPLE TRAVELLED FAR UNLESS – LIKE ANIMAL DROVERS AND TRADESMEN – THEY HAD TO.

EVEN BY THE 1780S, THERE WERE ONLY 400 STAGE COACHES SERVING THE WHOLE COUNTRY. THEY WERE KNOWN AS 'STAGE' COACHES BECAUSE EACH JOURNEY WAS MADE IN STAGES OF 10-15 MILES, AFTER WHICH THE HORSES WERE CHANGED. THE TOP SPEED WAS ABOUT 6 MILES AN HOUR. POOR SUSPENSION MADE TRAVEL UNCOMFORTABLE, PARTICULARLY IF YOU WERE IN A CHEAP SEAT ON THE OUTSIDE. IT'S WHERE THE EXPRESSION 'TO DROP OFF' (MEANING TO FALL ASLEEP) ORIGINATES.

GENTLEMEN

ENGLISH ROADS WERE ALSO NOTORIOUS FOR A VERY PARTICULAR HAZARD: THE GENTEEL HIGHWAYMAN. THERE ARE COUNTLESS STORIES OF POLITE ROBBERS APOLOGISING FOR THEIR DEEDS OR REDISTRIBUTING THEIR FRESHLY ACQUIRED WEALTH LIKE LATTER-DAY ROBIN HOODS. FOR MANY THEY BECAME CULT HEROES. THE EARLY FEMINIST MARY WOLLSTONECRAFT WROTE IN 1794: *'IN ENGLAND, WHERE THE SPIRIT OF LIBERTY HAS PREVAILED, IT IS USEFUL FOR AN HIGHWAYMAN, DEMANDING YOUR MONEY, NOT ONLY TO AVOID BARBARITY, BUT TO BEHAVE WITH HUMANITY, AND EVEN COMPLAISANCE.'*

WAR VETERANS

THE WORD 'HIGHWAYMAN' IS FIRST RECORDED IN 1617 AND MOST OF THE STORIES ABOUT THEM DATE FROM THE 17TH AND 18TH CENTURY. ONE THEORY IS THAT MANY ROYALISTS, HAVING BEEN TRAINED AS PROFESSIONAL SOLDIERS BUT DEPRIVED OF THEIR LAND AND WEALTH BY THE CIVIL WAR OF 1642-51, TURNED TO CRIME INSTEAD.

JAMES HIND (1616-1652) CERTAINLY FITS THIS PROFILE. HE WOULD INTERVIEW HIS CHOSEN VICTIMS BEFORE ROBBING THEM TO SEE IF THEY WERE SUITABLE TARGETS. *'NEITHER DID I EVER WRONG ANY POOR MAN OF THE WORTH OF A PENNY,'* HE INSISTED, *'BUT I MUST CONFESS, I HAVE MADE BOLD WITH A RICH BOMPKIN, OR A LYING LAWYER, WHOSE FULL-FED FEES FROM THE RICH FARMER DOTH TOO TOO MUCH IMPOVERISH THE POOR COTTAGE-KEEPER.'* HIND ALWAYS RETURNED SOME OF THE MONEY HE STOLE (EVEN FROM 'RICH BOMPKINS') TO COVER HIS VICTIM'S TRAVELLING EXPENSES.

CELEBRITIES

HIGHWAYMEN BECAME THE CELEBRITIES OF THEIR DAY, THEIR EXPLOITS CELEBRATED IN POPULAR BALLADS. ***GAMALIEL 'HOBGOBLIN' RATSEY*** (D. 1605) WORE A HIDEOUS MASK TO TERRIFY HIS VICTIMS AND WOULD SOMETIMES FORCE THEM TO PERFORM SCENES FROM SHAKESPEARE.

JAMES MACLAINE (1724-1750), WHO WORE A VENETIAN CARNIVAL MASK WHEN ABOUT HIS BUSINESS, WAS SO POPULAR HE RECEIVED 3,000 VISITORS TO HIS CELL ON A SINGLE SUNDAY.

THE CHERHILL GANG TERRORISED SALISBURY PLAIN BY HOLDING UP COACHES STARK NAKED.

MARCY CLAY (D. 1665) WAS TYPICAL OF THE SMALL BUT FAMOUS BAND OF HIGHWAYWOMEN. DISGUISED AS A MAN SHE HAD A REPUTATION FOR COURAGE AND SKILL WITH PISTOL AND SWORD. AMONGST THE MANY SHE ROBBED WAS HER OWN HUSBAND.

JERRY ABERSHAWE (1773-1795), THE 'LAUGHING HIGHWAYMAN', PAINTED CARTOONS OF HIS EXPLOITS ON THE PRISON WALLS WITH CHERRY JUICE AND HELD A FLOWER IN HIS MOUTH AS HE WAS WHEELED TO THE GALLOWS. HIS LAST ACT WAS TO KICK OFF HIS BOOTS. THIS WAS TO GET THE BETTER OF HIS MOTHER, WHO'D ALWAYS WARNED HIM HE WOULD *'DIE WITH HIS BOOTS ON'*.

GIBBET

FOR ALL THE FAME AND GLAMOUR, THE HIGHWAYMAN'S AVERAGE LIFESPAN WAS 28. MOST OF THEM ENDED THEIR LIVES AT THE GALLOWS, AFTER WHICH THEIR CORPSES WOULD BE HUNG IN A WIRE CAGE OR 'GIBBET' OFTEN AT A CROSSROADS AS A GRISLY WARNING TO OTHERS OF THE CONSEQUENCES OF CRIME.

BUT WHAT REALLY DID FOR THE 'GENTLEMEN OF THE ROAD' AS A PROFESSION WAS ECONOMICS. BY THE EARLY 19TH CENTURY, THE INTRODUCTION OF TURNPIKES (TOLLGATES) ON 20,000 MILES OF ROAD WAS GENERATING MORE THAN £500,000 A YEAR (ABOUT £75 MILLION IN TODAY'S MONEY). THE CASH WAS USED TO TRANSFORM THE SURFACE OF ROADS, MAKING COACHES FASTER AND LESS ACCIDENT PRONE. IT ALSO PAID FOR ARMED MOUNTED PATROLS, WHO PROTECTED THE TOLLGATES AND HUNTED DOWN MISCREANTS. THE LAST RECORDED CASE OF ROBBERY BY A MOUNTED HIGHWAYMAN WAS IN 1831.

STAND AND DELIVER

MOST OF OUR STOCK OF ROMANTIC HIGHWAYMAN CLICHES – MOONLIT ROADS, LONELY INNS, RUFFED SLEEVES AND SEXY 'MEN OF THE NIGHT' ORIGINATE IN A SINGLE POEM: ALFRED NOYES'S HUGELY POPULAR NARRATIVE BALLAD, *THE HIGHWAYMAN* PUBLISHED IN 1906.

'THE WIND WAS A TORRENT OF DARKNESS AMONG THE GUSTY TREES,
THE MOON WAS A GHOSTLY GALLEON TOSSED UPON CLOUDY SEAS,
THE ROAD WAS A RIBBON OF MOONLIGHT OVER THE PURPLE MOOR,
AND THE HIGHWAYMAN CAME RIDING – RIDING – RIDING
THE HIGHWAYMAN CAME RIDING, UP TO THE OLD INN DOOR.'

PROF. POTTS

Meet THE HORRIBLES

The Gaelic for hedgehog is *Grainneog*, or 'Horrible One'. Hedgehogs are not horrible at all, of course - they are, in point of fact, lovely - but they are certainly mysterious animals, little studied and widely misunderstood. Here is a selection of the not-very-much that is known about them.

If a hedgehog's attacked, the first thing it'll do is frown. Its frowning muscle – *panniculus carnosus* – runs all the way from its forehead to its tailbone. This contracts in 0.01 of a second, pulling its whole body into an almost impregnable ball. Rolling up completely is something hedgehogs don't often do. More usually, they'll just tuck their heads in and hunch their prickles over to protect their faces.

Humans (and not only those who live in caravans) have always eaten the 'hedgepig' or *furze-pig*. It's a free source of white meat that's relatively easy to catch. One account, published in 1699, recounts how the 'Moors of West Barbary' went about it: *'The Hedgehog is a Princely Dish amongst them, and before they kill him, rub his Back against the Ground, by holding its Feet betwixt two, as Men do a Saw that saws Stones, till it has done squeaking; then they cut its Throat, and with a Knife cut off all its Spines and singe it. They take out its Guts, stuff the Body with some Rice, sweet Herbs, Garavancas, Spice, and Onions; they put some Butter and Garavancas into the Water they stew it in, and let it stew in a little Pot, close stopped, till it is enough, and it proves an excellent Dish.'*

A persistent myth about hedgehogs is that if you remove their fleas, they'll die. In truth, they probably won't notice - they're indifferent to even the heaviest infestations. Since hedgehog fleas cannot live on humans, cats, dogs, or any other species, there seems no reason to inconvenience either the hedgehogs or the fleas.

Another myth is that hedgehogs are evolving to run away from cars...

...instead of rolling up. Hedgehog expert Pat Morris has shown that this would be quite pointless: a running hog is mathematically more likely than a stationary one to come under a vehicle's wheels.

Everybody knows hedgehogs hibernate in winter, but they don't actually need to. If there's food available, they'll stay active. New Zealand hedgehogs don't hibernate at all, and in Britain hibernation is becoming shorter (and rarer) because of mild winters. African desert hedgehogs avoid the killing heat by aestivating - that is, 'hibernating' during the summer.

African Pygmy Hedgehogs are the only kind known in the USA, and then only as pets. At the International Hedgehog Olympic Games spectators practice 'silent cheering' – waving their hands in the air by way of applause – so as not to startle the competitors.

At the Rocky Mountain Hedgehog Show in Denver, Colorado, quiet, calm hedgehogs tend to win the prizes. Sadly, the quieter the hog, the more likely it is to suffer from Wobbly Hedgehog Syndrome, which is similar to Multiple Sclerosis in humans. By selecting hogs that behave well for the show judges, pet owners have unwittingly created a population uniquely prone to this fatal and inherited condition.

Hedgehogs need open spaces to feed in. The golden age of the hedgehog in Britain began with the coming of the Romans - who first used hedges to divide fields - and lasted till after the Second World War, when intensive farming ripped hedges out to increase field sizes.

Between 1566 and 1863, hedgehogs were legally classed as vermin...

... due to the baffling belief that they stole milk from cows. Boys were encouraged to present severed hog-heads to churchwardens for a bounty of fourpence each; the rest of the animal could be eaten. One historian has estimated that from 1660 to 1800, 14,000 hogs a year died this way. Horrible! (Mind you, today 15,000 are killed on the roads each year...)

The greatest hedgehog mystery of all must surely be – what on earth are they doing on Christmas cards?

They are rarely seen in December, and have no known connection with the Christian nativity story, or with any other midwinter festival tradition. Presumably, they're there simply because they're lovely.

And *not* horrible.

ILLUSTRATION BY HUNT EMERSON

HIRSUTE HEBREWS

GROUCHO MARX (1890-1977) – COMEDIAN
Groucho's trademark moustache and eyebrows were fakes, drawn on with greasepaint to save him the bother of ungluing a false moustache night after night. His fast-talking wise guy emerged after his original German-accented character was booed during the anti-German sentiment of WWI. Without the moustache, Groucho was unrecognisable in public. He had fun with this, driving his wife to despair when waiting at busy restaurants for a table. She would implore him to tell the maitre d' who he was, at which point he would say: 'OK, OK. Good evening, sir. My name is Jones. This is Mrs Jones, and here are all the little Joneses.' When she begged he tell the truth, he appeared to relent and then said: 'My name is Smith. This is Mrs Smith, and here are all the little Smiths.'

HYMAN FISHMAN (1912-1976) – WRESTLER
Hyman Fishman was born in Massachusetts to Ukrainian immigrant parents. He began wrestling under his own name with other Jewish acts such as Abe 'Hebrew Hercules' Coleman and Herby 'Jewish Sensation' Freeman, whose ethnicity was a key part of their personae. There were even a few gentile wrestlers who advertised themselves as Jews, one being Paul Boesch, who was eventually outed by a Jewish reporter who saw him naked in a locker room. Hyman, barrel-chested and covered in hair, was nicknamed the 'Human Hair Brush'. Specialising in bear hugs, he reinvented himself as a Cossack called 'Ivan Rasputin' in a velvet cape with a bear on the back. Famed for his ability to rile a crowd, he was once brained by an irate showgoer with a monkey wrench.

GENE SIMMONS (1949-) – MUSICIAN
Born Chaim Witz in Haifa, Israel, Gene moved to New York City, aged 8, with his mother, Florence, a Holocaust survivor. At the industry launch of KISS in 1973, Gene, in full garb and make-up as 'The Demon', accidentally set his lacquer-coated hair ablaze during a fire-breathing stunt. In his first televised interview, he announced himself as 'evil incarnate', to which a fellow guest, comedienne Totie Fields, replied that it would be funny if, under all the make-up, he were 'just a nice Jewish boy'. Simmons' outrageous stage antics of tongue-waggling and spitting blood (yoghurt and food colouring) made the band a must-see attraction and the largest merchandising franchise in rock. KISS has licensed its name to over 2,000 products: action figures, lunch boxes, condoms - even a bespoke coffin called the KISS Kasket. A tireless but unmarried womaniser, Simmons has squired Diana Ross and Cher and now lives with an ex-Playboy Playmate. He speaks six languages.

SAMSON – JUDGE
Samson had perhaps the most crucial hairdo in history. As a Nazirite, dedicated to God from birth, Samson vowed never to cut his hair. In return, he was granted great strength to deliver the Hebrews from the Philistines. In the Bible, he rips a lion apart with his bare hands; sets fire to the tails of 300 foxes; and kills a thousand Philistines with the jawbone of an ass. The latter legend led the modern state of Israel to name its nuclear weapons programme 'The Samson Option'. When Samson trustingly divulged the secret of his strength to Delilah, she proved his undoing – though it was not she that cut his seven locks: a servant did the deed. Rastafarians cite the Nazirite vow as the reason for their dreadlocks: some believe Samson was dreadlocked himself.

GOLDA MEIR (1898-1978) – POLITICIAN
Born Golda Mabovitch in Kiev, Ukraine, her carpenter father moved the family to Milwaukee. In 1921, Golda left to live on a kibbutz in Palestine and threw herself into the Labour Zionist movement, often to the detriment of her family life. Her detractors called her 'The Mattress' for her numerous affairs with other activists. On 10 May 1948, four days before the declaration of independence, Golda traveled to Amman disguised as an Arab for a secret meeting with King Abdullah of Jordan to urge him not to join in an attack on Israel. When he asked her not to hurry to proclaim a state she replied: 'We've been waiting 2,000 years. Is that hurrying?' In 1969, at the age of 70, and secretly undergoing cancer treatment, Golda was called out of retirement to serve as Israel's fourth prime minister. Wire-wool haired and dowdy, her grandmotherly appearance belied her uncompromising toughness, earning her the moniker 'The Iron Lady' long before Mrs Thatcher.

HIRSUTE HEBREWS

MARK SPITZ (1950-) – SWIMMER

At the Munich Olympics in 1972, while other swimmers shaved their whole bodies, Spitz sported a fine moustache. He grew it to annoy his college coach (who specifically told him not to) and it took him four months. It didn't stop him winning seven gold medals – a record only surpassed in 2008 by Michael Phelps. When the Russian coach asked him whether it slowed him down, he replied: 'No, as a matter of fact, it deflects water away from my mouth, allows my rear end to rise and make me bullet-shaped in the water, and that's what has allowed me to swim so great.' The next year, every male Russian swimmer sported a moustache. Spitz retired aged 22. Two decades later he staged a comeback but was two seconds too slow to qualify for the 1992 Barcelona Games.

RON JEREMY (1953-) – PORN STAR

Ronald Jeremy Hyatt was born in Queens, New York to a middle-class Jewish family. He dropped his surname early on in his porn career after his grandmother, Rose (listed in the phone book as R. Hyatt), was inundated with phone calls from fans. His father told him: 'If you want to get into this naked, crazy business, so be it, but if you use the family name again, I'll kill you.' Since then, Ron, named 'The Hedgehog' for his paunchy hairiness, and 'Dong Juan' for his prized asset, has starred in and directed over 2,000 porn films and become the adult industry's most eminent ambassador. He was a consultant on the film 'Boogie Nights' and addressed the Oxford Union in 2005. His penis has its own Twitter feed.

KARL MARX (1818-83) – PHILOSOPHER

Marx was baptised a Christian aged 6, but came from a famous line of Rabbis dating back to the 16th Century. His father was the first man in the family not to become a Rabbi for generations, converting to Protestantism so he could legally practice law. In 1849, Karl moved to London with his wife Jenny. She called him her 'little wild boar', after the bristles that sprouted all over his body. He was a voracious writer but relied on his friend Engels for money. His mother complained that she wished he would make some capital instead of just writing about it and a friend once said she couldn't imagine him living happily under Communism. 'Neither can I', Marx replied. 'These times will come but we must be away by then.' A Prussian spy wrote of him: 'Washing, grooming and changing his linen are things he does rarely, and he likes to get drunk.'

HAREDI JEWS

Very orthodox Jews obey Leviticus 19:27: 'You shall not round the corners of your head, neither shall you mar the corners of your beard.' The first part is taken to mean that the hair at the temples shouldn't be cut: hence the dangling sidelocks or 'payot' worn by many. Adherents of Rabbi Nachman of Breslov wear them long because he promised that, after he died, he would use their payot to haul them out of purgatory. The second part is said to prohibit shaving with a blade against the skin but some hold that it's OK to snip the beard with scissors and much thought has gone into which brands of electric razors are allowed. Karl Marx's illustrious forebear, Rabbi Isaac Luria (1534-72) was said to avoid even touching his beard, lest he cause a single hair to fall out.

ALBERT EINSTEIN (1879-1955) – PHYSICIST

This picture was taken on Einstein's 71st birthday, when one too many photographers asked him to smile for the camera. He was constantly stopped on the street and asked to explain 'that theory', though it was not the Theory of Relativity that won him the 1921 Nobel Prize in Physics. (At the time, it was too controversial.) His public achievements as a physicist and an outspoken champion of pacifism and civil rights earned him 'Time' magazine's Man of the Century in 1999, but his private life was less admirable. His first marriage ended in a messy divorce, and throughout his second he remained very much a ladies' man. Offered the presidency of Israel in 1952, he turned it down saying: 'All my life I have dealt with objective matters, hence I lack both the natural aptitude and the experience to deal properly with people.' After his death, the pathologist at Princeton covertly removed Einstein's brain, hoping to uncover the secrets of his genius. It was only returned in 1998.

HA! HA!
BY ROBERT THOMPSON
NICE QUICHE, ARE THE KIDS NOT JOINING US FOR SUPPER?
HEN
Marvo
Contortionist
HOOVERING
LOOK, I DON'T WANT ANY TROUBLE, RIGHT?
HAMMER

MORE TEA!
HOLY SMOKE
HEAVEN
HEDGEHOG
GOSH, I DIDN'T REALISE IT WAS THAT HIGH
HIGH BARNET
HIMALAYAN
I say!
Toff
Leave it Terry he's not worth it.
HARD HATS

Health & Safety History of the World

In the beginning God created the heaven and the earth. And the earth was without form and void; and darkness was upon the face of the deep. And God said, Let there be light; and there was Light. And God saw the light, that it was dangerous; *and, lo, he took unto himself* protective glasses. *And God divided the light from the darkness using* extra thick scratch-resistant barrier tape. *And God said, Let there be* Health and Safety *and having* completed his maximum hours *he rested.*

THE BIBLE: *New Authorised Sanitised Sterilised Version* (Do Not Read)

13.5 BILLION YEARS AGO. The Universe is spontaneously created in the Big Bang. As time is also created at this moment, it has not been possible to prepare an Advanced Risk Assessment (ARA). Proceed with extreme caution.

4.5 BILLION YEARS AGO. Earth forms. As the molten ball cools, a solid crust quickly appears - which presents a tripping hazard.

3.7 BILLION YEARS AGO. Life appears. DANGER OF DEATH!

190 MILLION YEARS AGO. The therapsid proto-mammal Oligokyphus first suckles its young, entirely unaware that mammalian milk contains a source of phenylalanine.

400,000 YEARS AGO. Human precursor *Homo Erectus* harnesses fire. NO SMOKING. KEEP AWAY FROM NAKED FLAME. CONTENTS MAY BE HOT.

250,000 YEARS AGO. Evidence for cooking appears in Europe and the Middle East. Due to the lack of temperature control, food products may not be heated adequately. Make sure food is cooked and meat juices run clear.

40,000 YEARS AGO. Isotopic analysis of the skeletal remains of Tianyuan man, an early modern human from eastern Asia, identify him as the first man to have regularly fished and to be aware that fish can contain small bones.

20,000 BC. Humans in Southwest Asia and North Africa begin collecting wild seeds. Due to poor separation practices in the production line, meals may now contain nuts.

Lift heavy objects correctly

3,600 BC. The oldest freestanding buildings in the world are constructed at Ggantia in Gozo, Malta. The largest stones weighed over 50 tons and must be lifted with care.

3,400 BC. The Sumerians develop the first comprehensive writing script. From this date onwards it is essential to read ALL the instructions before proceeding.

No hard hat no job

1,200 BC. Trojan wars commence. From now on safety helmets must be worn.

DO NOT TURN PAGE WITHOUT ADULT SUPERVISION

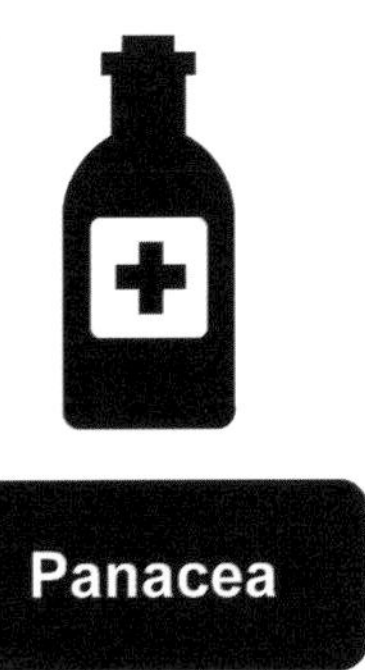

100 BC. In the absence of the poison labelling convention 'Not to Be Taken Internally' King Mithradates VI of Pontus derives a 'universal antidote' to poison, the *Antidotum Mithradaticum.*

80 AD. The punishment *Damnatio ad Bestias* is used to entertain the crowds at the inaugural games in the Flavian amphitheatre (Colosseum) in Rome. PLEASE DO NOT FEED THE ANIMALS. WILD ANIMALS ARE NOT PETS. DO NOT THROW COINS IN THE ALLIGATOR POOL.

6TH CENTURY. St Piran, patron saint of tin miners, floats from Ireland to Cornwall on a millstone. Not To Be Used As A Life Preserver. No Swimming Outside Flags. Follow instructions on tin.

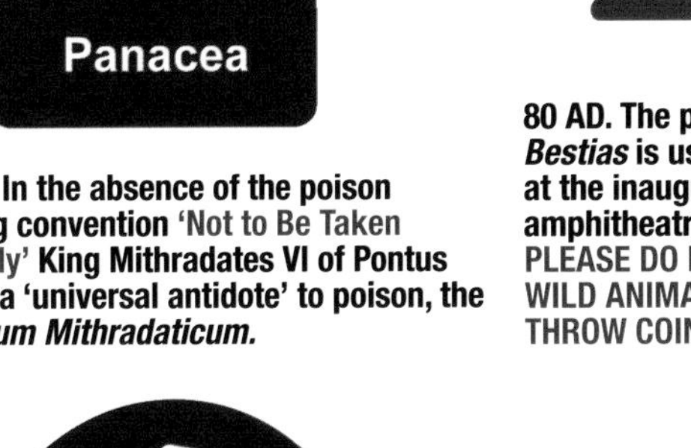

1206. Arab inventor Al-Jazari describes a flushing toilet mechanism. Caution Wet Floor. Now wash your hands.

1492. The first scouts sent out by Columbus in Cuba describe tobacco use amongst the native peoples, causing them to exclaim 'Fumar puede reducir el flujo sanguinea y provoca impotencia!'*

**Smoking can reduce blood flow and cause impotence.*

1720. Collapse of the South Sea Bubble ruins thousands of people including the composer George Frideric Handel with care, proving that the value of your investment may go down as well as up.

Warning
Mind your head

1792. Highwayman Nicholas Jacques Pelletier ignores the beware sharp edges sign and becomes the first man to be executed using the Guillotine.

Caution
Raw meat

1821. Melville writes *Moby Dick* after hearing how George Pollard's ship is sunk by a rogue whale and his crew survives for 94 days by resorting to cannibalism, which can only help you lose weight as part of a calorie-controlled diet.

1830. William Huskisson fails to realise that the approaching train is not scheduled to stop at this station and is run down by Stephenson's 'Rocket'.

1897. J.J. Thomson discovers the electron, proving once and for all that everything in the entire universe contains small parts and may present a choking hazard.

1902. More than 30,000 people are killed in the eruption of Mont Pelée in Martinique after failing to heed warning signs such as WHEN RED LIGHT SHOWS WAIT HERE.

1965. Swedish engineer Sten Gustav Thulin invents the lightweight plastic shopping bag and the KEEP AWAY FROM SMALL CHILDREN label.

2011. Climate change, air pollution, global terrorism, viral pandemics, pit-bull terriers, volcanic ash and the risk of being crushed by a block of frozen urine the size of a piano which has escaped from an aircraft toilet mean that, now more than ever, **IT IS DANGEROUS TO LEAN OUT OF THE WINDOW.**

HOT DOG
EATING STYLES
by Brian McFadden
THIS COMIC MAY CONTAIN: SNOUTS, OFFAL, ANUSES, AND TRACE AMOUNTS OF ONE CLUMSY SLAUGHTERHOUSE EMPLOYEE.

THE HAZMAT

THE DOUBLE BARREL
I HATE MY GUTS.

THE COLLATERAL DAMAGE
SMACK!

THE PARTY CLOWN
OH, HI! I MADE A CUTE WIDDLE GIRAFFE FOR YOU!
NOW EAT IT!

THE CANNIBAL
I'M DELICIOUS!

THE TRICKLE DOWN DOG
YOUR PROCESSED MEAT, MADAME.
NOW MAY I ATTEND MY MOTHER'S FUNERAL?

HOT DOG CART HOT TUB
HOT
DOGS
HOT
COME ON IN! THE HOT DOG WATER'S REVOLTING!

NOAH'S CONDIMENT ARK
I COMMAND THEE, ALL OF MUSTARD-KIND, BOARD MY WEENIE, IN THE NAME OF TASTINESS!

HOT OR NOT?

Finding the right partner can be a rewarding way of passing the time in between splitting up, but how can you be sure that he or she is 'The One'? Especially if they've been under the sod for hundreds of years... Try our vacuous quiz!

Girls first...

1. Tired of muscle-bound hunks, you ache for someone with a mind like a clear, deep pool. A Greek guy called Socrates asks if you fancy an evening at Walthamstow dogs. He's a legendary figure in Western philosophy but would you be seen dead with him? **HOT** or NOT?

2. You're sitting in a bar weeping into a Bacardi Breezer over the wreckage of your love life when your best mate offers to set you up with an 18th-dynasty pharaoh friend of hers. Tutankhamun is 17, rich, and revered as a god. But is he right for you? **HOT** or NOT?

3. You've been doing Shakespeare in Lit class when the teacher asks if you'd like a blind date with Richard III. To be honest, the ranting megalomaniac didn't come over too well in the play, but maybe he's got a different kind of hump in mind? **HOT** or NOT?

4. There's a new guy on your fave dating website and he sounds like a dream! His chat handle is Giacomo, he's from romantic Venice, he knows all the A-list celebs of the 18th century and he runs the state lottery. Could this be your Casanova moment? **HOT** or NOT?

5. In an act of desperation you've agreed to meet an actor friend-of-a-friend for a drink after his play. He's got great reviews and, supposedly, a magnetic personality. The name – John Wilkes Booth – rings a bell, but should you give him a buzz? **HOT** or NOT?

Now the boys...

6. You're in the rugby club bath blagging about all the royals you've slept with when one of the lads suggests a threesome with Cleopatra. You remember from Asterix books that she was quite a turn-on, but what if she's got a face like Grant Mitchell? **HOT** or NOT?

7. You get an email from Sparta. Someone called Helen has seen your profile and wants to be your friend. She's a Bronze Age babe, so won't share your passion for the X-box, but she's launched a thousand ships on Facebook. Does she float your boat? **HOT** or NOT?

8. You're a shipmate on HMS *Vanguard* in the Bay of Naples in 1799 when Admiral Nelson's lover Lady Emma Hamilton signals that she's gagging for it. Do you turn a blind eye or do you allow her to pipe you aboard and then run her up your flagpole? **HOT** or NOT?

9. You've always had a bit of a thing about nurses so when Florence Nightingale invites you round for a game of hospital corners you have fantasies of the young Babs Windsor before she was in *Eastenders*. Are you up for rubbing the Lady's Lamp? **HOT** or NOT?

10. You're Best Man at a wedding and the groom tips you off that there's an old Queen making eyes at you. Boudica mints her own money (something even Cheryl Cole can't do) and she's waiting for you behind the Karaoke machine. **YEA** or NAY?

Hot or Not? The Answers...

1. Socrates (c. 469 BC–399 BC) **NOT!**

You should love someone for their mind and there is a lot of mind to love with Socrates, but this fella was no oil painting. According to one of his best friends, Alcibiades, he looked like a statue of Silenus, an obese old man in Greek myth with the ears of a horse. In Aristophanes' play Clouds (423 BC), he's described as pale and thin from strain and deprivation, dirty and hungry, with long straggly hair. Rather you than me!

2. Tutankhamun (1341 BC – 1323 BC) **NOT!**

Oh dear, another wrong turn. Tutankhamun might have ruled Egypt, but DNA and CT scans have shown that he suffered from malaria and a bone disorder. Carsten Pusch, a geneticist at the University of Tübingen says he was 'a frail, weak boy who had a bit of a club foot and who needed a cane to walk'. And the age difference may prove insurmountable – not only is he barely legal, but he's been dead for over 3,000 years.

3. Richard III (1452 – 1485) **HOT!**

Richard III wasn't grossly deformed. Shakespeare's source was Polydore Vergil, a contemporary of the king but the paid spin-doctor of his deadly enemy and successor Henry VII. At the time, physical appearance was thought to be good indicator of personality, so Vergil made Richard ugly and crippled to show that he was mentally unfit. Most contemporaries said nothing about his appearance: he could well be fit.

4. Giacomo Girolamo Casanova de Seingalt (1725 – 1798) **NOT!**

He might have made a reputation for himself as a ladies man, but that was obviously with the lights firmly OUT. By early middle age he had smallpox scars, sunken cheeks, a hooked nose and was frequently bankrupt from gambling debts. Quite apart from the fact that he caught venereal disease eleven times, his friend Prince Charles de Ligne said of him 'He would be a good-looking man if he were not ugly.' Blech!

5. John Wilkes Booth (1838 – 1865) **HOT!**

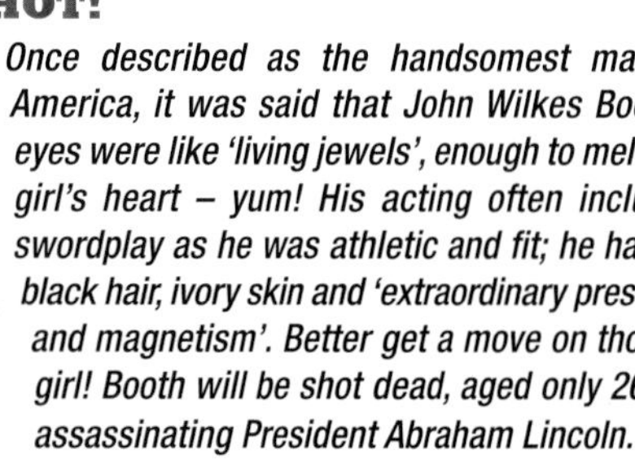

Once described as the handsomest man in America, it was said that John Wilkes Booth's eyes were like 'living jewels', enough to melt any girl's heart – yum! His acting often included swordplay as he was athletic and fit; he had jet black hair, ivory skin and 'extraordinary presence and magnetism'. Better get a move on though, girl! Booth will be shot dead, aged only 26, for assassinating President Abraham Lincoln.

6. Cleopatra VII Philopator (69 BC – 30 BC) **NOT!**

No one who knew Cleopatra ever commented on her beauty, although many say she was charismatic and clever – so if you're reading this you're probably out of luck there anyway. The discovery of a silver coin in 2007 bearing likenesses of Antony and Cleopatra shows her with a shrewish profile and him with bulging eyes, a crooked nose and a bull neck. She was also already married – to two of her little brothers.

7. Helen of Troy (probably mythical) **HOT!**

'Phwoarr!' as they say in the Athenian agora. Helen of Troy was born from an egg after Zeus seduced her mother in the guise of a swan. According to the Roman writers Ovid and Sextus Propertius, she wrestled naked and went hunting topless. She was so gorgeous that 99 wealthy men fought for her hand and when Paris stole her from her husband Menelaus it started a war that lasted ten years and killed thousands. Yessss!

8. Emma, Lady Hamilton (1761 – 1815) **NOT!**

When the painters George Romney and Joshua Reynolds picked Emma as a teenage model for their paintings she was an exotic dancer and a real looker, but sadly she let herself go. In 1796, the Viceroy of Corsica said of her: 'Her person is nothing short of monstrous for its enormity.' Later, a Swedish diplomat commented: 'she is the fattest woman I've ever laid eyes on' and Lady Elgin bitched: 'She is indeed a Whapper!'

9. Florence Nightingale (1820 – 1910) **HOT!**

Florence was possibly the cleverest woman of her age, but more importantly than that she was a stunna - lively, beautiful and passionate. She took after her mother, Fanny, whose looks were legendary, and she was fluent in French, German, Italian, Latin and Greek, which she owed to her father, who also taught her mathematics, philosophy and history. So she won't enjoy your footie stories: in fact, she's way out of your league.

10. Boudica (d. AD 60 or 61) **NOT!**

Seriously frightening. According to the Roman historian Dio Cassius she was 'possessed of greater intelligence than often belongs to women. In stature she was very tall, in appearance most terrifying, in the glance of her eye most fierce, and her voice was harsh; a great mass of the tawniest hair fell to her hips...' She burned London and St Albans to the ground and the Welsh knew her as 'Buddug'. Fail!

HONEY

The delicious dribble of Hymenoptera*

Nothing but money is sweeter than honey.
BENJAMIN FRANKLIN

MOST BEES DON'T MAKE HONEY

There are 20,000 species of bee in the world, but only 6 of them produce honey.

Honey comes from wasps and ants

Native Americans eat honey-making ants. They put them rear-end first into their mouths, bite into their gigantically swollen abdomens and suck the honey out. In Mexico, wasps are commercially farmed for honey: they eat the whole wasps (lightly toasted) there too.

Bears don't like honey

In some places, bears are a serious pest for beekeepers – but they aren't after honey. They tear the hives apart with their claws to get at the highly nutritious baby bees.

SMOKING BEFORE MEALS

Bees are traditionally pacified with smoke, but it doesn't make bees drowsy (as many people think), it makes them panic. They eat all the honey they can, ready to flee, but this makes them too fat, full and content to be bothered with much in the way of stinging.

FROM THE JAR OF THE BOTTOM

All honey (whether from bees, wasps or ants) is essentially vomit, but the rare and expensive 'honeydew' honey comes from the anal secretions of sap-sucking insects.

STICKY BEE-SUIT

The best armour for honey-hunters is – honey. Smear yourself in it, and any bees that land on you will tuck in instead of stinging you. Apparently. To be honest, none of the Elves here in the QI Toadstool were willing to personally verify this.

Honey is the best medicine

The antibacterial qualities of raw honey have been used since ancient times to heal wounds and bruises but new research shows that New Zealand Manuka honey is even effective against the deadly MRSA, which is resistant to the most powerful antibiotics.

BEES AREN'T BUSY

In all cultures throughout history, the bee has been a symbol of industrious activity but the truth is that up to two-thirds of a honey-bee's life is spent doing absolutely nothing, just mooching about the hive, humming aimlessly.

Bzzzz Bzzzz Bzzzzzz
Bzzzzzz Bzzzz
Bzzzzz
Bzzzzzzzzzzzzzzzz

HONEY-HUNTING

The San Bushmen of the Kalahari follow flying bees until they see some going in the other direction. This tells them they've walked past the nest, so they turn round and track the bees back the way they've come. The African honeyguide bird (*Indicator indicator*) leads humans and other mammals to a bees' nest, waits politely while they open it up and take out the honey, and then steps into the hive and eats the wax.

**The order of insects containing all the 130,000 known species of bees, ants and wasps.*

IN HELMAND

ROSS NOBLE

IN DECEMBER 2009, ROSS WENT TO AFGHANISTAN TO DO FOUR SHOWS TO ENTERTAIN THE TROOPS.

Flying in a Hercules is brilliant.

So they can avoid getting shot at, they turn off all the lights and fly up high like and at the last minute swoop down and then come in and land. The seats are like bench seats, so instead of facing forward you and all the troops are sat in a big long line and all the baggage is just shoved in a big cargo net on the back. I have seen the future of Easy Jet and Ryan Air…

What was weird about Helmand for me was the fact that it sounds so much like Hellman's. You know, Afghanistan produces a lot of heroin and I had this idea that the troops weren't there to liberate the people but to wrestle control of the world's mayonnaise – trying to cut it off at source so it doesn't flood illegally into America.

The news gives you the idea that there are like primitive tribesmen armed with rocks fighting against these high-tech planes that drop stuff, but it's not like that at all. It's young kids – teenagers – walking around villages where guys who look like farmers suddenly shoot at them. As soon as they try to deploy any sort of military tactics, the guy throws his machine gun in a ditch and picks up a shovel, and they can't shoot him. They're not allowed to open fire on places of worship, so you have Taliban guys standing in the doorways of Mosques firing at them. There are constant casualties, but they don't report them. They just patch the kids up and send them back out there…

It's a place where Health & Safety doesn't exist. Well I say that, right, but actually it does. Obviously everyone there is wearing beige clothes, all the buildings are beige and the desert is beige and so everything is the same colour, especially at night. And some of the vehicles are so big that if the driver accidentally knocks someone over, he sometimes has no idea he's even done it. So now at night everyone has to wear reflective bands, like cycling bands, so the drivers can see them in the dark. But they're wearing camouflage! People in full camouflage wearing high-vis jackets!

They have heaps of Heath & Safety rules - that's the bizarre thing - that they are really strict about. Before you go and have your dinner there are basins outside the food tents to wash your hands, and it's all disposable plates, plastic cutlery. When you finish, you take your plate, walk out and it goes straight in the bin. There's no washing up. Outside the gate there's some guy with an old rocket launcher ready to blast you and the roads are full of explosives. Yet, inside the gate on the other side there's a sign that says, 'If you walk along here you must have a harness,' or 'you can't climb a ladder', or whatever.

I didn't get any heckles. Well, I watched what I said. You don't really want to take on a thousand trained killers, y'know? One of the guys in the audience had been shot earlier that day. His plane wasn't going to leave until after the show, so he was all bandaged up and waiting in a hospital bed. But he said he wasn't going to sit in a hospital bed bored out of his mind if there's a show on - so they picked him up and carried him down. They got some cushions from the NAAFI and stuck him in the front row. He was off his face on morphine and completely white and just sat there with his flesh wounds. It's quite a different thing when you do a show and the front row was shot that morning. There's a different vibe, y'know. So I didn't get heckles – it was more moans of discomfort.

Afterwards a guy came up to me, he was a bomb disposal officer. He'd been out all day, lying in the dust on his stomach disarming improvised explosive devices and he said 'Bloody hell Ross! Stand-up comedy! That must be the hardest job in the world!' And I said, 'Er… just think through what you've said there a minute…'

The Special Forces have their own 'hermetically sealed' compound away from everyone else. They have their own vehicles and they put tarpaulins over them so that they can't be identified. One lad, a regular squaddie, came into the compound on an errand and he saw all these tarpaulins. He's going, like 'What do you have under there?' And the Special Forces guy says: 'I can't tell you that.' There's so much mystery and myth about the SAS (which they love) because the stuff they do is so incredible. So the lad asks: 'Is it something a bit special?' 'Yes', says the Special Forces guy, 'we have actually got invisible cars…' 'Wow!' says the squaddie. 'Yeah' says the guy. 'Trouble is, we have to put tarpaulins over them, otherwise we can't find them in the morning…'

Fear is only really the processing of the unknown. If you jump off a high diving board or you go on a roller coaster you are fearful the first time, but the second time you know what to expect. So, whenever I do anything that's scary, I think 'what is this similar to? What experience have I had like this that didn't kill me?' But out there in Helmand, er, I couldn't think of one…

ROSS NOBLE
DONATED HIS FEE
TO HELP
FOR HEROES.

If you'd like to contribute too, you can visit this page
www.helpforheroes.org.uk

A typical, traditionally woven Afghan carpet. (Look carefully at the contemporary design.)

HOLY RELICS
The alleged TRUE CROSS was kept in Jerusalem until its loss in 1187
"RELIC" comes from the Latin "reliquus" meaning ~something left over~
~GENERAL FRANCO~ owned an arm of St. Theresa of Avila. He kept it with him for the rest of his life and died clutching it.
SAINT ANTHONY is the patron saint of lost objects. His tongue is kept in Padua
In the Middle Ages monks at Canterbury would water down blood supposedly taken from St. Thomas Becket to sell to pilgrims.
ST. HUGH, shown an arm of St. Mary Magdalene in Provence, tried to cut a lump off with his knife to take home with him. When this failed, he chewed a piece off with his teeth and carried the morsel home.
IN THE MIDDLE AGES MANY CHURCHES KEPT THE VIRGIN'S BREAST MILK. JOHN CALVIN SAID THAT "HAD MARY BEEN A COW ALL HER LIFE SHE COULD NOT HAVE PRODUCED SUCH A QUANTITY."
PAPAL BULL
ST LUKE was a Syrian. His body is in Padua~ but his head is in Prague.
In Cologne there is a chest said to contain the remains of the Three Wise Men.
MARY'S GIRDLE
~THE~ 30 PIECES OF SILVER
JESUS' UMBILICAL CORD
Thomas' FINGER
A CRUMB FROM THE SERMON ON THE MOUNT.

THE HOLY PREPUCE

JESUS' FORESKIN

JESUS' FORESKIN, OR 'HOLY PREPUCE' WAS A RELIC FOUND ALL OVER EUROPE IN THE MIDDLE AGES. ONE RECENT STUDY COUNTED 21 DIFFERENT CLAIMANTS.

SAINT BIRGITTA claimed that the Virgin Mary wore Jesus' foreskin as jewellery for her whole life.

LEO

THE 1ST KNOWN HISTORICAL MENTION OF THE FORESKIN CAME IN 800, WHEN THE HOLY ROMAN EMPEROR CHARLEMAGNE GAVE IT TO POPE LEO II AS A PRESENT.

MEDIEVAL SCHOLARS WERE CONCERNED: JESUS HAD ASCENDED BODILY INTO HEAVEN BUT THE FORESKIN REMAINED ON EARTH. WAS JESUS THEREFORE IN HEAVEN WITH A CIRCUMCISED PENIS? SOME ARGUED THAT IT WOULD HAVE FLOWN UP TO JOIN HIM IN HEAVEN, FLUTTERING LIKE A BUTTERFLY

St. Catherine of Siena had a vision in which she wore the foreskin as a wedding ring in her marriage to Christ.

ST. BRIDGET SAID SHE HAD RECEIVED BITS OF FORESKIN FROM AN ANGEL WHICH SHE PUT ON HER TONGUE GIVING HER ORGASM-LIKE SENSATIONS.

Austrian mystic Agnes Blannbekin had a vision where she **ate** it.

By the 20th century only 4 foreskin relics remained ~ 3 in Rome and the "true" foreskin in Calcata, Italy. The Catholic Church was hugely embarrassed: The prepuce was said to be an "irreverent curiosity" and mention of it became a punishable offence. The Calcata foreskin was stolen in 1983. The Catholic Church wasn't entirely sad to see it go.

BY CHERRY DENMAN

HARRY HOUDINI

He escaped from prisons naked, from coffins...

THE LEGENDARY ESCAPOLOGIST HARRY HOUDINI (1874-1926) WAS BORN ERIK WEISZ IN BUDAPEST AND WAS THE MIDDLE OF SEVEN CHILDREN. HIS FAMILY WERE HUNGARIAN JEWS WHO CHANGED THEIR SURNAME TO WEISS (AND ERIK TO EHRICH) ON MOVING TO AMERICA WHEN HE WAS FOUR. HIS AMERICAN FRIENDS CALLED HIM EHRIE, OR 'HARRY'.

Houdini's childhood was tough – he had almost no formal education, instead selling papers and shining shoes on Milwaukee street corners. He once saw a board advertising a job at a tie manufacturer with a queue of people outside. He walked to the front of the line, took down the board, told everyone the position had been filled, and then walked in holding the board and got the job.

He was obsessed with magic and locks from an early age. He named himself after Robert-Houdin, the great 19th century French magician. He added the 'i' to make 'Houdini' because his partner, Jake Hyman (together they were 'The Brothers Houdini'), told him that in French it would mean 'like Houdin'. He was also known as 'Eric the Great', 'Mysterious Harry' and 'The King of Cards'.

Houdini's first performance seems to have been at the age of nine, when a visiting circus paid him thirty-five cents to hang upside down and pick up needles with his eyelashes. Another version of events says he started at the same age as a trapeze artist, under the title 'Eric, Prince of the Air'. Before he was famous, Houdini and his wife spent years half-starving in poverty while he performed as The Wild Man, sitting in a cage and tearing at raw meat.

On achieving fame, Houdini escaped from prisons naked, from coffins, from paper boxes without damaging them, from iron boilers, from government mailbags and from the belly of a whale. He once escaped from a Siberian prison van, for which the only key was at the far end of Russia. Had he failed, he'd have had to travel all the way there to be released.

He was thrown into rivers in chains, or buckled into straitjackets while hanging by his ankles upside down from skyscrapers. He challenged police to handcuff him to pillars in their cells, and escaped almost before they reached the door.

On stage, he would free himself from the audience's chains and locks in three minutes and spend half an hour or so behind a screen reading the paper. He then doused himself with water (to look like sweat) and emerged victorious.

His assistants were totally loyal to him. One of their jobs was to deal with punters who showed up in the wings and wouldn't be deterred – they were knocked out and woke up elsewhere later. Houdini carried at least fifteen pairs of handcuffs with him when he travelled. He hid lock-picks in his hair, in his throat, even buried in the thick skin on the soles of his feet.

He lured his audiences with the slogan 'Bring Your Own Padlocks' (later, his assistants swapped them for easier ones) and his posters showed seven bald men with the letters H-O-U-D-I-N-I on their scalps. One of his favourite tricks was the 'milk can', in which he escaped from a specially modified milk churn full of water (he could hold his breath for three minutes). When he emerged, the churn was still full of water and none of the locks had been disturbed.

Houdini was obsessed with death. He bought Edgar Allen Poe's writing desk and the original electric chair and loved visiting the graves of dead magicians. He nearly died when he was buried alive, manacled, under six feet of earth. He panicked, tried to dig himself out and shouted, but his mouth filled with earth. Eventually, he burrowed his way out - but he never tried the stunt again.

... from iron boilers, from government mailbags and from the belly of a whale.

He was fascinated with murderers like John Wilkes Booth, who shot President Lincoln, and Charles J Guiteau, the American lawyer who was hanged after assassinating President Garfield. Locked naked in the place where Guiteau had awaited execution on Death Row, Houdini not only got out himself but freed all the other men and then locked them up again in the wrong cells.

Houdini attended séances in a false beard and glasses and exposed fake mediums by tearing off his costume at a crucial moment. He even bought a spiritualist church and the title of Reverend to expose swindling psychics. To show how fraudulent mediums worked, he wired up his house to eavesdrop on his guests and then amazed them by revealing facts about them.

Houdini was a close friend of Sir Arthur Conan Doyle, despite the fact that he believed in fairies and lectured on spiritualism. Maddeningly, Sir Arthur was convinced that Houdini was a medium without knowing it, though Houdini insisted it was all a trick. When Houdini died, his distraught wife held séances to try to contact him with no success.

He married his wife Bess two weeks after meeting her. They were married three times –on Coney Island, in a Catholic ceremony, then by a rabbi. She was always his assistant on stage. They were besotted for thirty years. He wrote her hundreds of letters, notes and postcards, often from a different room in the same house. They called each other 'Mr. Houdini' and 'Mrs. Houdini'.

When they argued, Houdini would leave, walk round the block, then return and throw his hat into the room. If it was thrown out again she was still angry.

They had no children, and deeply regretted it. Instead Houdini created a dream child called Mayer Samuel, and sent his wife daily reports on his progress. They stopped when Mayer became President of the United States.

Houdini adored flying and was one of the first to make a controlled, powered airplane flight in Australia. He learnt to fly in 1909 in Germany, on condition that he taught German Army officers how to fly. When World War I came, he was furious with himself that he had put countless enemy pilots into the air.

All his life Houdini wanted to be an American. He even tried to sign up to fight in World War I – as Harry Handcuff Houdini – despite being 44. Rejected on age grounds, he contented himself with doing a huge amount of free entertainment for the troops. His favourite trick was 'Money for Nothing', producing an endless stream of coins for US soldiers out of thin air. He gave away over $7000 of his own money (perhaps $200,000 today) in this way.

Houdini is usually said to have died from a punch in the stomach from an American student trying to prove his strength, which brought on a fatal attack of appendicitis. The night after being punched, Houdini had stomach ache and, a few days later, was diagnosed with acute appendicitis. But you can't get appendicitis from a punch to the stomach. It seems Houdini already had the condition and assumed the pain was due to being punched. In any event, he refused to see a doctor until his wife insisted. He survived the removal of his appendix but died a week later, on Halloween 1926, in spite of the doctor predicting he would live no more than twenty-four hours.

Two thousand people attended his funeral. As the coffin was lowered into the grave, one of the pallbearers whispered to another:

'Suppose he isn't in it...!'

Phill Jupitus

The History of

THE FIRST EVER HAMSTERS WERE THE VAST AND TERRIFYING **MUROIEA COLOSSII**, WHICH WEIGHED 8,000 TONS AND COULD GET A TYRANNOSAURUS IN EACH CHEEK... HOWEVER, THEY WERE SO CUTE THEY THOUGHT HAVING SEX WOULD BE WRONG, WHICH WAS WHY THEY BECAME EXTINCT...

CAVE PAINTINGS AT **LASCAUX** IN FRANCE MAKE REFERENCE TO THE HUNTING OF DEER AND WHAT SEEM TO BE BEARS, BUT ARE ACTUALLY HAMSTERS... THIS PHENOMENA IS DIRECTLY THE RESULT OF POOR PERSPECTIVE SKILLS BY THE ARTISTS AND EARLY CAVE HAMSTERS GETTING IN THE WAY...

VIKINGS USED KINDLY FACED HAMSTERS AS A WAY OF ALLEVIATING POST TRAUMATIC STRESS AND WOULD ALLOW THEM TO NEST IN THEIR BEARDS... A WELL KNOWN NORSE APHORISM WAS – **"IF I DO NOT MEET YOU IN VALHALLAH, MAY YOUR BEARD REMAIN SWARMING WITH HAMSTERS...**

IN **ELIZABETHAN** TIMES BEFORE PRINT BECAME COMMONPLACE YOU COULD BUY A SMALL REPLICA OF THE GLOBE THEATRE, CONTAINING A TROUPE OF COSTUMED HAMSTERS TO RE-ENACT SHAKESPEARE PLAYS... THEY PROVED SO POPULAR THAT VENDORS URGED THE BARD TO CHANGE ONE ENDING SO GERTRUDE **EATS** HAMLET...

PRIOR TO THEIR FIRST MANNED FLIGHT IN 1783 THE **MONTGOLFIER BROTHERS** LAUNCHED A SERIES OF TEST BALLOONS FILLED WITH HAMSTERS... THESE WERE DEVOURED BY KESTRELS WHICH WOULD END UP STUCK IN THE BASKET... FOR MONTHS, ETIENNE MONTGOLFIER FEARED THAT FLIGHT TURNED YOU INTO A FAT KESTREL...

NAPOLEON BONAPARTE DID NOT CONSOLIDATE A POSITION OF ADVANTAGE AT THE BATTLE OF BORODINO IN 1812, AFTER PERFORMING A 'DRY RUN' WITH 50,000 HAMSTERS... SADLY MOST OF THE 'FRENCH HAMSTERS' ENDED UP BEING DEVOURED BY FERAL CATS WHICH HE TOOK AS A BAD OMEN...

Hamsters

THE PYRAMIDS AT GIZA ARE AGREED TO BE THE FIRST ARCHITECTURAL DISASTER, AS THE DESIGNER HAD INTENDED THEM TO BE A SMALL STONE HABITAT FOR THE PHAROH'S HAMSTERS... AN ENRAGED CHEOPS INSISTED THAT THE CONTRACTORS FINISH BUILDING THE PYRAMIDS AS A FORM OF PUNISHMENT...

IN ROMAN TIMES, HAMSTERS WERE CONSIDERED TO BE A DELICACY AND A CHEF'S SKILL WAS MEASURED BY THEIR ABILITY TO TRAIN DOZENS OF HAMSTERS TO CRAM THEIR POUCHES WITH HERB STUFFING AND SULTANAS BEFORE ROLLING IN SEASONED FLOUR AND DIVING INTO VATS OF HOT OIL...

IN 16TH CENTURY PORTUGAL, HAMSTERS WERE TAKEN ON LONG OCEAN VOYAGES AS A LIVE FOOD SOURCE... THIS IS HOW THEY WERE ACCIDENTALLY INTRODUCED TO THE FOOD CHAIN ON MAURITIUS, EVENTUALLY WIPING OUT THE DODO WHICH TURNED OUT TO BE THE HAMSTERS NATURAL PREY...

IN THE EARLIEST COLONIES IN AMERICA THE HAMSTER WAS A FORM OF CURRENCY USED WITH INDIGENOUS PEOPLE... THE GOING RATE WAS TWENTY HAMSTERS TO THE TURKEY... RHODE ISLAND WAS PURCHASED BY THE PILGRIM FATHERS FOR 2 SACKS OF HAMSTERS...

VICTORIAN ENGINEER ISAMBARD KINGDOM BRUNEL WAS NOTED FOR HIS EYE CATCHING STOVEPIPE HAT... FEW KNEW THAT IT PROVIDED A HOME FOR UP TO 15 HAMSTERS AT A TIME... HE DREW UP PLANS FOR A THIRTY TON CAST IRON WHEEL IN 1858 JUST A YEAR BEFORE HIS DEATH...

IN 1888 IT IS ALLEGED THAT VAN GOGH SEVERED HIS OWN EAR IN AN ACT OF LOVELORN MADNESS. ONE RECENT THEORY POSITS THAT IT WAS CUT OFF IN A FIGHT WITH GAUGIN... THE TRUTH IS THAT IT WAS GNAWED OFF BY HIS OWN HAMSTER 'GAUGIN' BECAUSE HE WORE A DODO BASED FRAGRANCE...

‘Never trust a man who, when left alone in a room with a tea-cosy, doesn’t try it on’. BILLY CONNOLLY

The earliest record of humans wearing hats comes from a cave at Lussac-les-Châteaux in central France. The rock drawings are 15,000 years old and we’ve been putting things on our heads ever since.

Hats

BLACK HAT

The Bowler hat, the traditional symbol of London commuters, began life as a riding helmet. It was designed in 1849 by London hatmakers Thomas and William Bowler as a tough, low-rise hat to protect the heads of mounted gamekeepers from low-hanging branches. Its practicality and strength made it the hat of choice for cowboys in the American west, where it was known as the *derby*. After British railway workers were seen wearing it to Peru and Bolivia in the 1920s, Quechua and Aymara women adopted it as part of their national dress, renaming it the *bombin*.

SMART HAT

Students of the medieval theologian John Duns Scotus (1265-1308) first wore the ‘dunce’s’ hat. His name means ‘Scottish John from Duns’ (a village in the Borders) and the idea was to funnel divine wisdom into the head. But the followers of ‘the Subtle doctor’ gained a reputation for pointlessly abstract arguments about the existence of God and the ‘thingyness’ of things. By late 16th century, their headgear had become associated with foolishness.

FLAT HAT

The beret (from Latin *birretum*, meaning a small, hooded cloak) started out as a Pyreneean shepherd’s hat. In 1918, the British Tank Corps trained with the French regiment, the *Chasseurs Alpins*, who had adopted blue berets in the 1880s because they were warm and weatherproof. Close-fitting and with no peaks to snag on things, berets were perfect for tank crews. They were also cheap to make, didn’t show sweat stains and were easy to carry (they fit snugly under an epaulette). This has made them the universal hat for the modern soldier.

SUN HAT

In the nineteenth century, there was no standard headgear for US baseball teams. Sports fans struggled to distinguish their favourite player under the assortment of straw boaters or cotton hats worn to provide shade from the sun. The classic ‘Brooklyn’ cap with its large brim or ‘bill’ was first worn in 1860 by the Brooklyn Excelsiors amateur team and others followed suit. In 1954, it became the iconic ‘59Fifty’ cap worn by official baseball teams (beloved of rednecks, hiphop stars and chavs). All authentic 59Fiftys come from a single family-owned company – New Era Cap Co, Inc of Buffalo, NY.

'If you want to get ahead, get a hat'

ADVERTISING SLOGAN 1920s

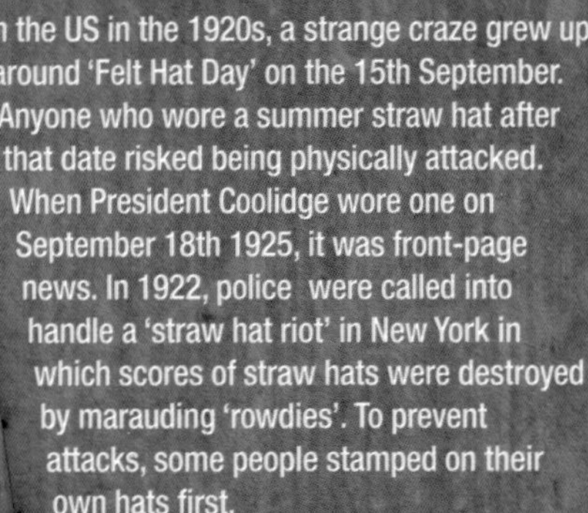

MAD HAT

In the US in the 1920s, a strange craze grew up around 'Felt Hat Day' on the 15th September. Anyone who wore a summer straw hat after that date risked being physically attacked. When President Coolidge wore one on September 18th 1925, it was front-page news. In 1922, police were called into handle a 'straw hat riot' in New York in which scores of straw hats were destroyed by marauding 'rowdies'. To prevent attacks, some people stamped on their own hats first.

OLD HAT

The modern sense of 'out of date' was first recorded in 1911. It once meant something rather different. Grose's *Dictionary of the Vulgar Tongue* (1796) defines 'old hat' as 'a woman's privities, because frequently felt.' Hat felt was made from beaver or rabbit fur that had been ground, squeezed and heated.

BAD HAT

The Royal Society for the Protection of Birds began as an alliance of anti-plumage pressure groups. Volunteers targeted any woman who appeared in church on Sunday wearing a feather in her hat and sent her insulting letters telling her that she was supporting animal cruelty. These various factions joined together to create the RSPB. In the 1880s, at least 5 million wild American birds were killed each year for hat trimmings.

HIGH HAT

The tall chef's hat or *toque blanche* traditionally had a hundred pleats to represent the number of ways an egg could be cooked. *Toques* (from the Arabic *taq* for 'round'), were originally short and black and worn by French magistrates. The inventors of French *haute cuisine* (and of kitchen hygiene) Marie-Antoine Caréme and Auguste Escoffier adopted them, making them white for cleanliness and tall to make it clear who was boss – literally *chef*.

'I myself have 12 hats, and each one represents a different personality. Why just be yourself?'

MARGARET ATWOOD

NO HAT

Most people stopped wearing hats after the World War 2. No one knows why. New hairstyles, the rise of the car, demobilization - even the new fashion for sunglasses – all took the blame for the sudden abandonment of the hat. At first, the hat industry thought 'hatlessness' was a passing fad and newspaper reports of 1948 bemoaned the new 'barehead' fashion. People who dared to walk hatless through the hat-making towns of Denton and Stockport risked being abused by factory workers who saw their livelihoods disappearing.

'Cock your hat – angles are attitudes'.

FRANK SINATRA

Heaven
I'VE GOT A TERRIFIC LAWYER!
TESCO
BLOODY ARCHITECTS!
I'VE ALWAYS FANCIED LIVING IN A GATED DEVELOPMENT!
THIS IS THE AUSTRALIAN SECTION
VIP AREA
I'M AN EX-MP. THAT'S MY SECOND CLOUD
CCTV
GREAT. NO DISABLED ACCESS!
Newman

HELL
HANDCART PARKING
CLAMP
TESCO
AT LAST - THAT BARBECUE SUMMER THEY PROMISED US!
BP
...AND HERE'S ME AND MARJORIE IN MAJORCA....
HOLIDAY SNAPS
ENGLAND V GERMANY WORLD CUP
IT COULD BE WORSE - IT COULD BE HULL!
HELL-O!
SATAN SHOWS US ROUND HIS LOVELY 7TH CIRCLE
IN CASE OF NO FIRE BREAK GLASS
THE BEAST'S NOT WHAT I EXPECTED
666

Happy Potter and the Deathly Hangover

Johnny Vegas makes a 'Morning After' teapot

Johnny recommends 3 magic cures for feeling like death

The Full English

Pickled sheep's eyeballs

Dried bull's pizzle

PHOTOGRAPHY BY ANDY HOLLINGWORTH

Johnny is now as perky as a spring chicken that's just spent the night with a defibrillator.
He adores clay
And finds pottery a deeply sensual experience
Johnny has a degree in Art & Ceramic Design from Middlesex University
He also makes Bulls' Pizzles
Le Marquis de Mud
Chuffin' Nora!! That's not a teapot – it's a flowerpot!
Back to the treadle, or 'nodger' as it's known in Stoke*
*No it isn't.

The completed 'quobble' – technical potter's term for an unfired, spoutless teapot without a lid or handle*

Potticelli's 'The Mirth of Vegas'

Johnny has a teapot on display in the V &A. It was made in under a minute. This one's much better – it took about 4 hours

You can see the finished teapot on eBay. We're going to auction it to the highest bidder (closing date 31 January 2011) and give the money to Adopt A Potter

Adopt A Potter is a charity that puts young people through pottery school for a year. Without it the world will soon run out of hand-made jugs and things.

To bid for Johnny's teapot go to eBay and type the word 'quobble' in the search box

***As far as we know, there isn't a word for one of these – but there should be.**

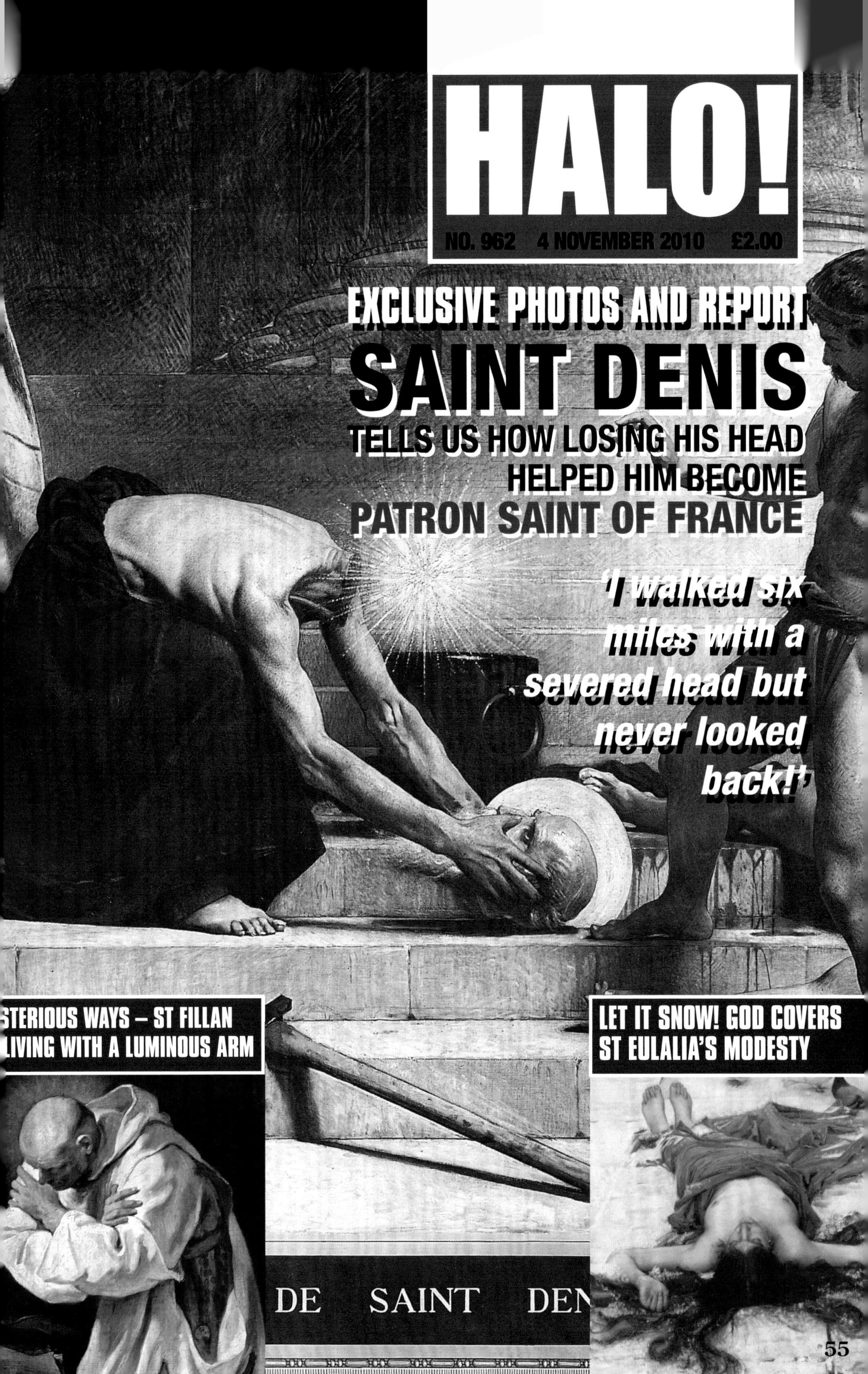
HALO!
NO. 962 4 NOVEMBER 2010 £2.00
EXCLUSIVE PHOTOS AND REPORT
SAINT DENIS
TELLS US HOW LOSING HIS HEAD
HELPED HIM BECOME
PATRON SAINT OF FRANCE
'I walked six miles with a severed head but never looked back!'
STERIOUS WAYS – ST FILLAN
LIVING WITH A LUMINOUS ARM
LET IT SNOW! GOD COVERS
ST EULALIA'S MODESTY
DE SAINT DEN

Saints Alive!

We monitor the ups and downs of the hottest celebrity saints around

MILK AND HONEY

St Colman of Ela finds being a foster father easier than most – 'For I have two paps such as no saint ever had before, a pap with milk, and a pap with honey, and these I will give them.' Move over ladies, this is a man's job!

HALO! HALO! HALO!

It looks like the Romans got there first again. Here's Neptune, God of the Sea, sporting his very own halo – and not a Christian martyr in sight.

Better Than Two

Bringing up three baby boys is no picnic, but thanks to God's gift of a third breast St Gwen the White has never been happier. 'Now they call me Alba Trimammis!'

I didn't ask to be cured!

St David seems to have rushed in where angels fear to tread, infuriating the hermit St Kyned of Wales by curing his lameness without asking first. But quick-thinking St Kyned has the answer. Before St David can say 'No need to thank me' he's on his knees praying to have his crippling problem back.

And who is God to say no to a request like that?

CEPHALOPHORE CONUNDRUM

Saint Valerie of Limoge, St Paul of Tarsus and Saint Ginés de la Jara face every cephalophore's (head carrier's) nightmare. 'When I'm depicted carrying my head under my arm, where should artists draw my halo?' Don't ask us Val – we're stumped!

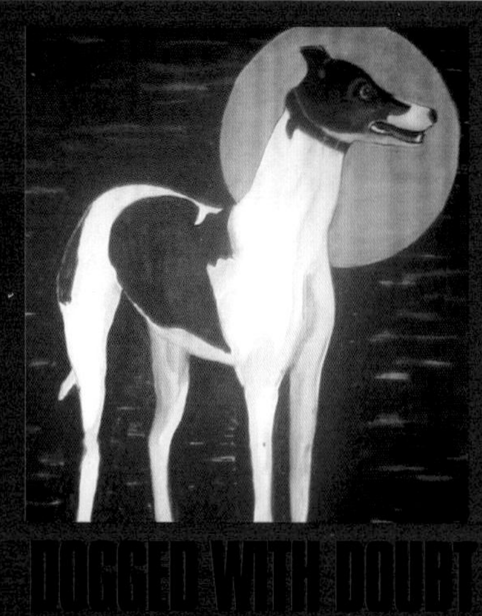

DOGGED WITH DOUBT

It's no easy ride for Saint Guinefort, the miracle-working 13th century French dog. Having been wrongly beaten to death by his master who thought he'd eaten his baby son, he was venerated as a saint. But now the church says 'No'.

'Outside of my frankly backward neighbourhood nobody seems to take me seriously.'

HUNDREDS AND HUNDREDS

A GOOGOL IS 1 FOLLOWED BY 100 ZEROS. A googolplex is 10 to the power googol, a number larger than all the hydrogen atoms in the observable universe. To write it down would take up more space than the universe currently occupies.

Larry Page and Sergey Brin, founders of Google, copyrighted the word after looking to see if 'googol' was taken as a domain name as it summed up the projected size of their database. Fortunately for them, they misspelled it.

Legend has it that the Century Plant (*Agave Americana*) blooms once every 100 years. In fact, it takes 10-15 years. It grows up to 26ft (8m) tall and in Mexico its acidic sap is made into a 1,000-year old alcoholic drink called pulque.

When Mark Twain died in 1910, he left behind a 5,000-page autobiography, asking for it not to be published until 100 years after his death. That time has now come: the first volume is due to be published in the same month as this *QI Annual*. The book is said to be scandalous and feature vibrating sex-toys.

Escaping from exile on Elba, Napoleon returned to France to try and regain power. Britain, Russia, Austria and Prussia pledged 150,000 men each to defeat him, which they did at Waterloo - after his '100 Days' of freedom.

Tony Hart, who invented the animated clay character Morph, created the ship on the *Blue Peter* badge. He was paid a flat £100 fee for his design.

In a 1987 study, just 100 surnames accounted for 85 per cent of the Chinese population. According to the 1990 census, the most common was Li. It's shared by over 100 million Chinese: more than the population of Germany.

Hundred, West Virginia, is named after Henry Church who lived to be well over 100 (109). Seen snoozing on his porch, passing train conductors would point out 'Old Hundred'. The name stuck and the town was named after him.

A species of salamander called the Olm, nicknamed the 'Human Fish' after its fleshy skin, can live to be 100 years old - far longer than any other amphibian. Scientists have no idea why. Olms come from Southern Europe, are roughly a foot (30cm) long, blind and live in complete darkness.

In Greek myth, Argus had 100 eyes. The goddess Hera sent him to guard Io, whom she had turned into a cow to stop her husband Zeus fancying her. Zeus had Argus killed but Hera put his eyes on the peacock's tail as a reward.

The largest bank note in England is the 100 million pound note, called a Titan. It is only used inside the banking system and there are only 40 in existence.

When Pythagoras discovered that the square of the hypotenuse of a right-angled-triangle equals the squares of the other two sides, he is said to have celebrated by sacrificing 100 oxen to the Gods. Such sacrifices were known as hecatombs and were a popular tradition in Ancient Greece and Rome.

UNHUNDREDS – THINGS THAT DON'T AMOUNT TO 100

The 100 Years' War (1337-1453), which lasted 116 years

Roman Centurions, who usually only commanded not 100 but 80 men

Centipedes, none of which have ever been found with 100 legs

Napoleon's 100 Days, which were actually 111 days

ILLUSTRATION BY MORGAN RITCHIE

HËNJ

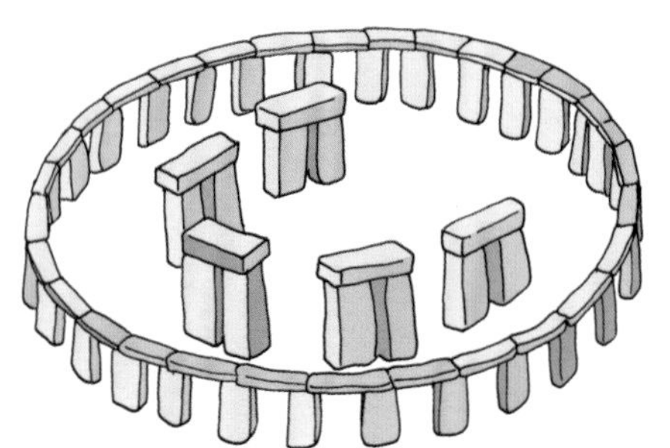

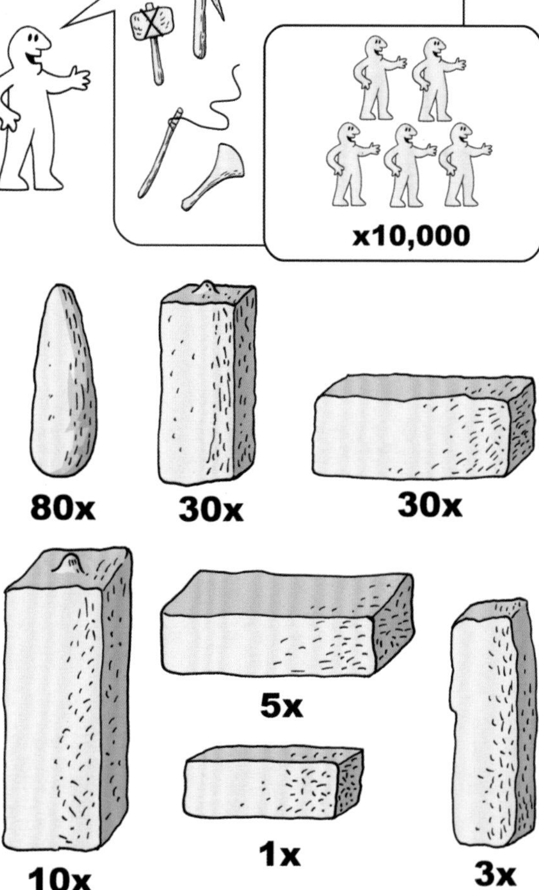

1

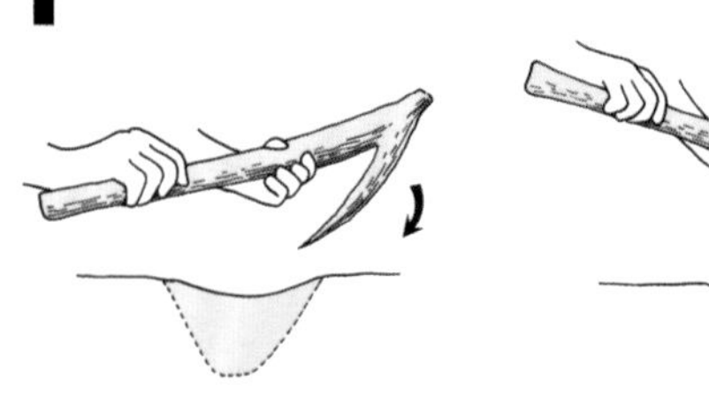

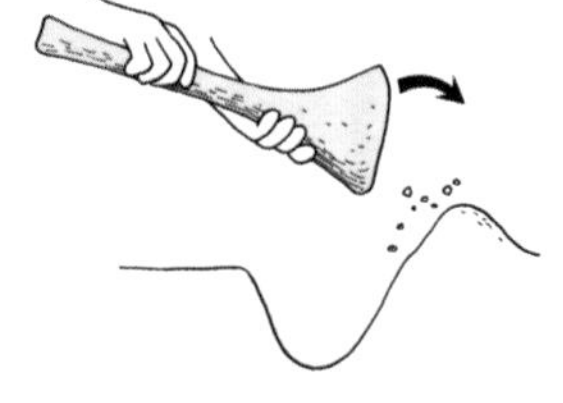

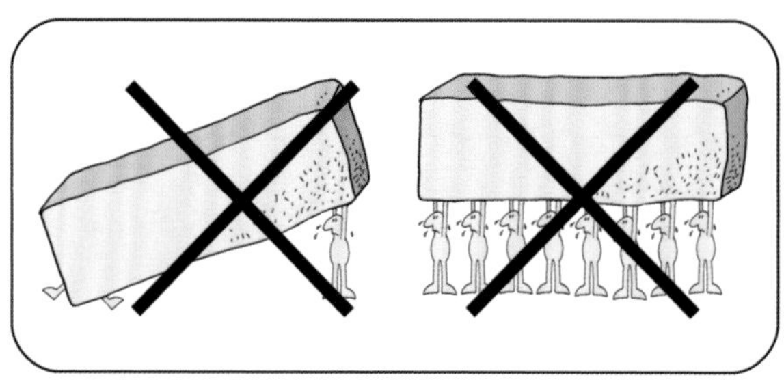

2

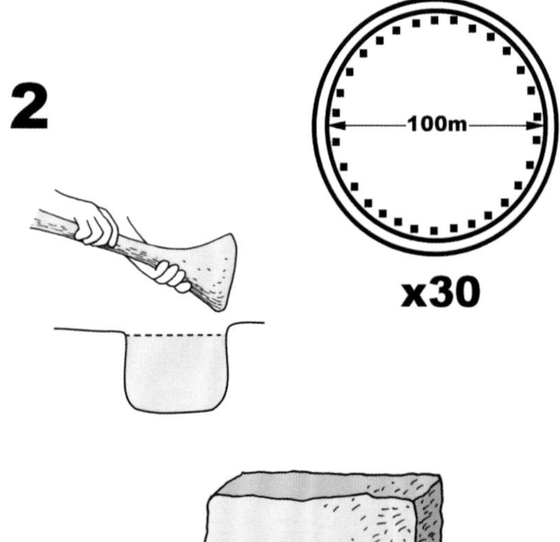

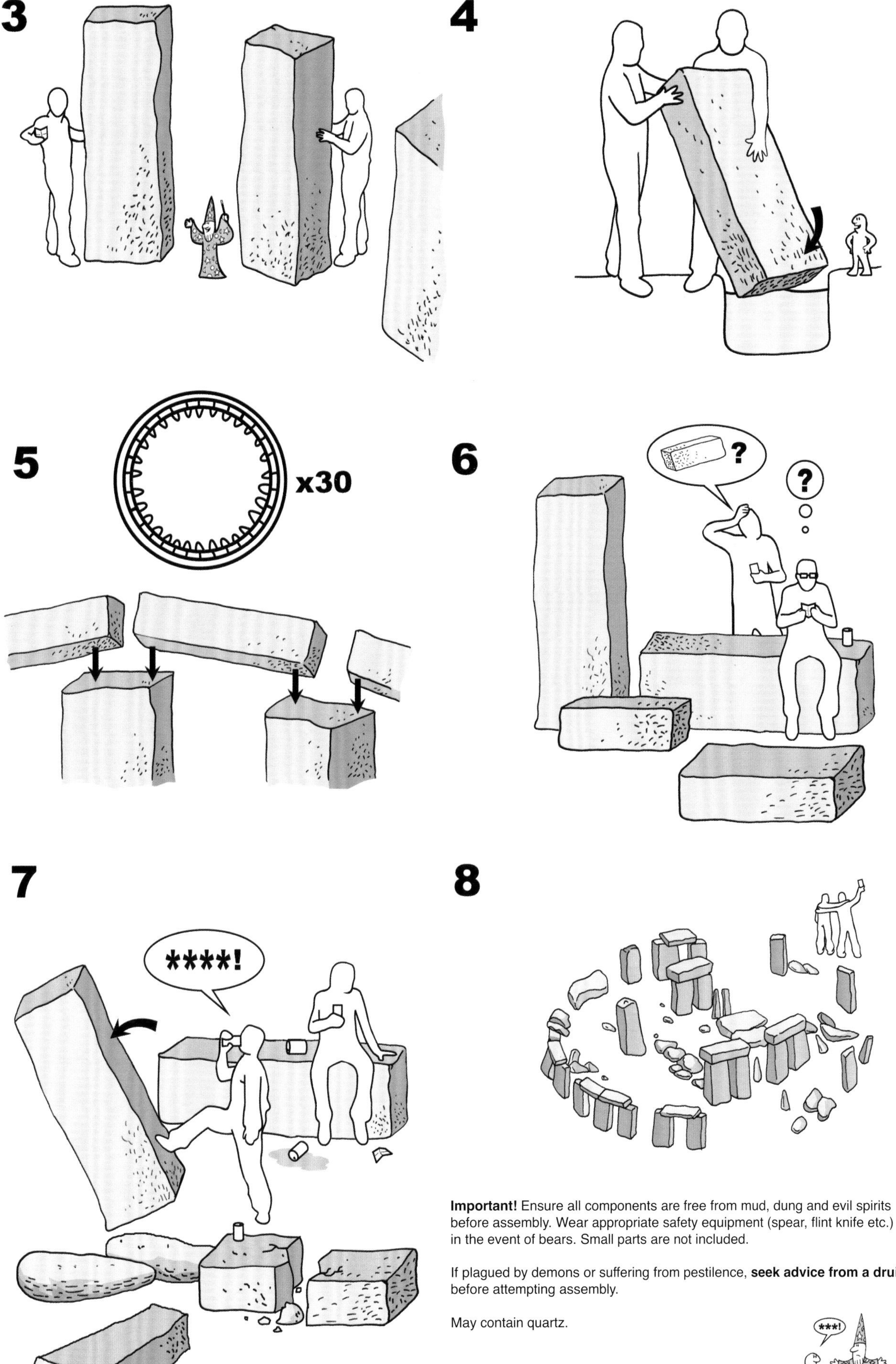

Important! Ensure all components are free from mud, dung and evil spirits before assembly. Wear appropriate safety equipment (spear, flint knife etc.) in the event of bears. Small parts are not included.

If plagued by demons or suffering from pestilence, **seek advice from a druid** before attempting assembly.

May contain quartz.

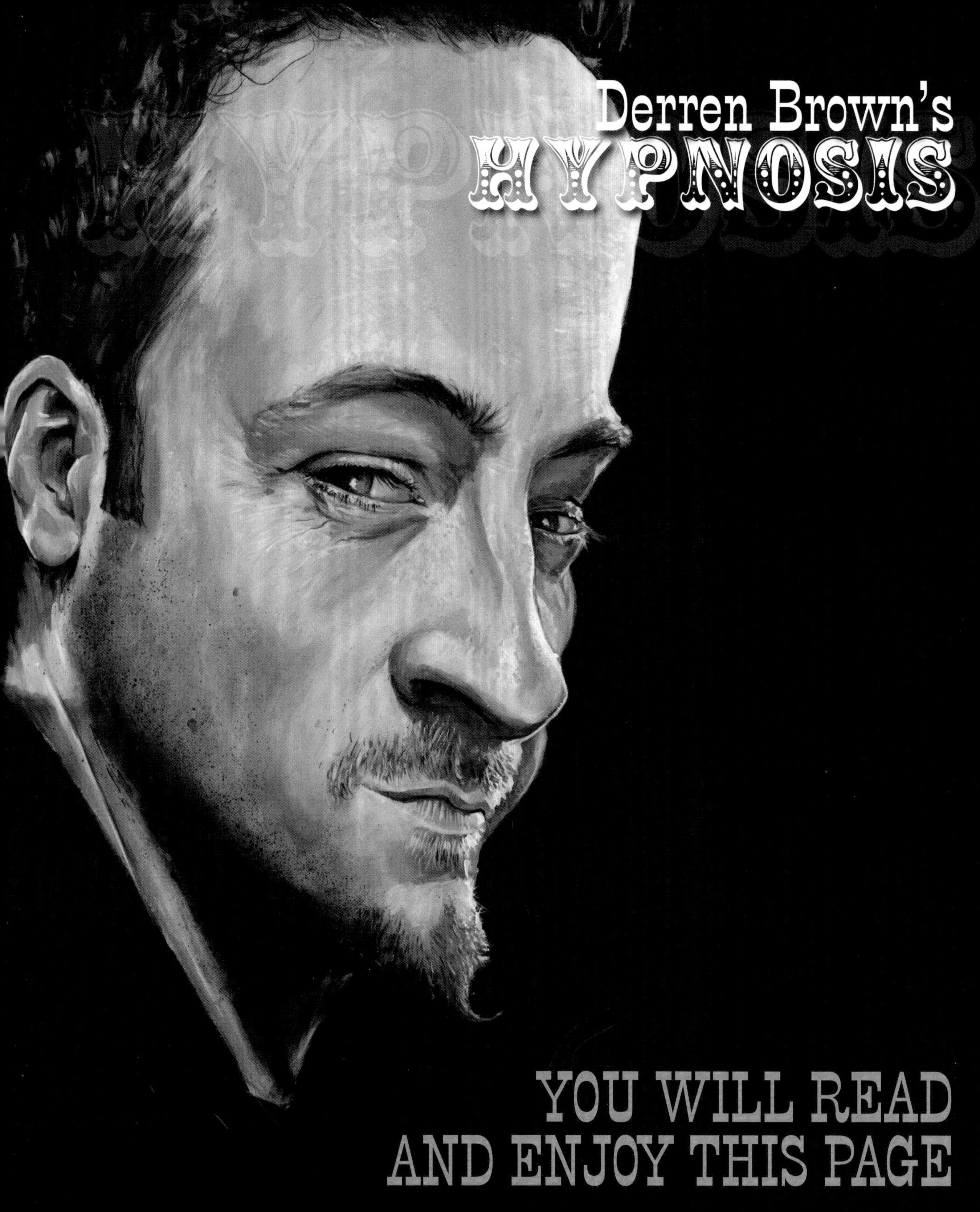
Derren Brown's
HYPNOSIS
YOU WILL READ
AND ENJOY THIS PAGE

FRANZ MESMER (1734-1815) was a flamboyant, purple-robed physician who believed there were magnetic and spiritual forces in the universe that he could move around by making 'mesmeric passes' - and thus cure ailments. This was first done with magnets, and later just with his hands. Though his theories have been found to have no substance, from him we have inherited many romantic notions of hypnosis, as well as all sorts of nonsense about the therapeutic power of magnets and the laying on of hands to heal. He did, however, produce results – just not for the reasons he thought. Typically his clients were sexually suppressed Victorian women: having them lie in a bathtub of iron filings and rubbing their thighs with a rod did indeed cause many of them to convulse and emerge feeling better, but supernatural forces had nothing to do with it. Later, a Scottish surgeon called **JAMES BRAID** (1795-1860) looked more carefully at what actually made it all tick, exploring the idea of suggestion, and first giving us the term 'hypnotism'. At last it could be looked at rationally, and therefore more usefully. Interestingly, it was associated for a while with either epilepsy or 'nervous hysteria' (a mental condition supposedly confined to women, derived from the Greek word for 'uterus'). Many phenomena associated with hypnosis today (such as zombie-like states and catatonic or 'rigid' bodies) are a hangover from this early confusion.

What is hypnosis? What isn't it?

Here are some facts and fancies…

Hypnosis is quite a recent thing.

False. 'Hypnosis', or something very like it, has existed since human beings first experimented with altered states of consciousness or tried to influence others around them.

The hypnotised subject is not in control.

False. On stage, it looks as if the subjects are puppets obeying the will of the showman, but the reality is less straightforward. The more suggestible or 'open' personalities enter imaginatively into the idea that they have 'succumbed' to the power of the hypnotist, and act out his instructions because it is the easiest thing to do. In a therapeutic situation, it's even less true: the client is actually *given back* control over an area where he or she has become stuck in unhelpful behaviours.

Things can be done under hypnosis that can't be done normally.

False. People can be made to feel strange things (such as a chair being boiling hot), but our senses fool us all in normal life when the conditions are right. Hypnosis can be used to control pain, but we've all had the experience of cutting ourselves and not feeling pain until we see what we have done, or not realising how much we need to go for a pee until we get home and can't find our front door keys. There is no hypnotic phenomenon, no matter how remarkable it may appear, which cannot be re-created outside of a hypnotic state through such ordinary devices such as suggestion, hype and the exercise of charisma.

Everyone can be hypnotised.

True-ish. We all respond to suggestion to some degree and in certain contexts – especially with authority figures such as doctors, teachers and parents. The hypnotic 'trance' – which is really just a state of concentration and relaxation as found in deep prayer, daydreaming or meditation – is something we can all enjoy. A smaller number of people – normally around a third - will find themselves 'good subjects' for a hypnotist. The best are those who are most open and responsive in everyday life; those who are closed off and cynical tend to be more difficult to reach. Animals can also be 'hypnotised'. Flip a rabbit on its back, hold it firmly in position with its head back for a couple of minutes, and you'll find it will become perfectly motionless and unresponsive, until you clap your hands loudly above its head. Take a chicken, hold it firmly with its beak down and focused on a chalk line and it will do the same. A dog (and many wild animals) will seldom attack if fixed with a direct gaze.

People can't be made to do things they don't want to do.

True. Except that you *can* make them *want* to do that very thing. The rather brilliant *Derren Brown: The Heist*, which you will go out and buy three copies of later today, was an experiment in how to get people to the point where they would commit what they believed to be a violent crime, without ever directly telling them to do it.

People don't know what's going on when they're hypnotised.

False. The subject is aware of everything. And almost everybody can remember it all afterwards.

There's no such thing as hypnosis.

True *and* false. 'Hypnosis' is no one specific thing: it's more of a shorthand word for a type of experience rather like stage magic. The 'magic' occurs in the mind of the audience: we know what we mean when we say it but it doesn't describe what the magician is doing (which may be a combination of a number of things). The definition of hypnosis can be very wide: some would say that to be wholly absorbed by a speaker is to be 'hypnotised'. Looked at like that, hypnosis certainly exists as a feeling of complete relaxation and concentration, and is more common than we might think. The typical demonstrations of the stage hypnotist, on the other hand, are really only the creation of a context wherein people are given permission to behave responsively and engage their imaginations. There is no 'special state' or 'power' to speak of. In that sense, hypnosis doesn't exist at all.

Sleeeeeeeep

HIPSTERS
A cultural analysis

by JEN SORENSEN

THE RISE OF GEEK CHIC

With the nerd look being extremely 'in' these days, it can be tricky to differentiate hipsters from the un-hip.

This young woman has taken geek chic to the next level, with orthodontic headgear serving no practical purpose whatsoever.

SPECTACLE SEMIOTICS OF THE HIPSTER FEMALE

Neo-schoolmarmism has been the dominant aesthetic for many years (see 'nerd look,' above).

More recently, the '80s revival has inspired some women to adopt enormous, face-dwarfing glasses in alarming colours.

NOTE: Sarah Palin's angular frames are not to be confused with hipster glasses. When in doubt, examine context. Hipsters are rarely Bible-thumping wackadoodles.

FACIAL HAIR SEMIOTICS OF THE HIPSTER MALE

The scraggly hipster beard is the new frontier in cool for men tired of emo fashion.

As always, there are some who take the look too far.

**70s rock star turned outdoorsman and gun nut. Google him and give yourself a fright!*

ACCIDENTAL HIPSTERS

Anthropologists have recently identified this important related phenomenon.

This pensioner unwittingly purchased a pair of Nike Dunks without any comprehension of their vintage hip-hop symbolism.

This insurance salesman wore his gold-rimmed aviator shades for so long that they eventually became cool again.

This knitting grandmother is strangely unaware of her place in the D.I.Y. craft movement.

This farmer is tragically unconscious of the fact that his entire wardrobe is a goldmine of proletariat kitsch.

JEALOUSY

LUST

DECEIT

VANITY

ALTRUISM

COURAGE

LEADERSHIP

INTUITION

I'm childish?!... Huh, you're a million zillion times more childish than me

IMMATURITY

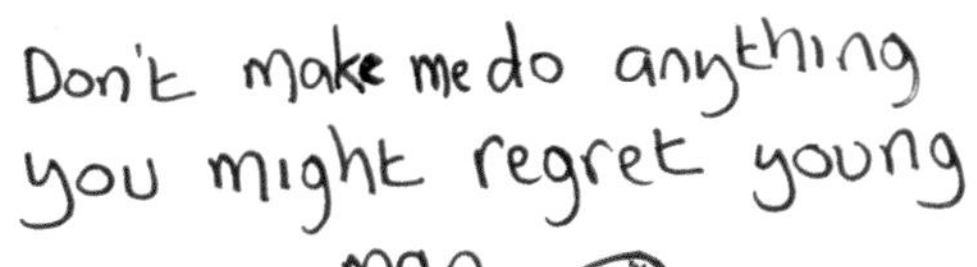

OPTIMISM

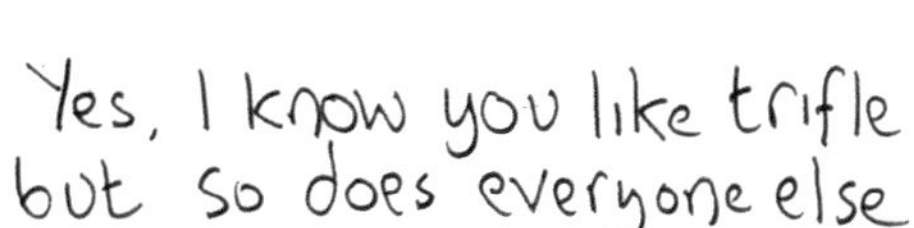

GREED

SELFISHNESS

HUNTING BY TONY HUSBAND

Not the most adventurous of hunters was he?

Isn't that the breed whose parents are very protective?

Oh not bloody Mammoth again!

Come in, I won't eat you

Oh dear, this could be awkward

HUNTING
AND FIELD SPORTS

WORDS BY SIMON EVANS
ILLUSTRATION BY GUY VENABLES

The collective noun for hunters, dating back to 1486, is a 'blast'. The *Oxford English Dictionary* gives it as obsolete, but it shouldn't be. And now it isn't.

In the early days of the American frontier, the skin of a male deer was worth $1 – hence the term a 'buck' for a dollar bill.

In 1800, there were an estimated 30 million bison on the plains of the American mid-west. A hundred years later, after the longest and wildest spree of unchecked hunting in history, there were less than 1,000.

When women rode to hounds sidesaddle, the rider put one leg around a horn attached to the saddle so that both her legs were on one side of the horse, with one foot in a single stirrup. As a respectable woman always had to cover her ankles, if she fell off, her long dress often caught on the saddle horn and dragged her along behind the horse. The introduction of the 'safety skirt' in 1875 was intended to prevent this. This was loosely fastened to both the woman's waist and the saddle, so that, in the event of a fall, it came off the woman and remained attached to the saddle, leaving the lady in question in a pair of breeches. Initially regarded by many as tasteless and indecent, in 1884 the Quorn hunt made them compulsory on the grounds that 'better a live lady in breeches than a dead one in a habit'.

In the early 1800s, landowners resorted to increasingly barbaric deterrents to protect their game. Mantraps were designed to clamp onto the poacher and had names like modern day wrestlers: 'The Crusher', 'The Body-squeezer' and 'The Thigh-cracker' were top sellers. Spring guns were heavily loaded pistols hidden in a tree with the trigger attached to a tripwire. Unfortunately, the poachers, knowing the land better than either its owner or the gamekeepers, would find the traps and re-set them elsewhere. In 1821, the three sons of Admiral Wilson of Redgrave Hall in Suffolk went out hunting with a boy. All four were shot and badly wounded when one of their dogs touched the wire of a single spring gun.

Specialist shooting shops sell all manner of fancy hunting accessories, including containers for a wide range of alcoholic beverages, taken to sustain the 'guns' during their labours from mid-morning onwards. You can get silver or pewter hipflasks for cognac, malt whisky or cherry brandy; silver-plated sloe gin cups; fluted solid-silver vintage champagne beakers; or, for those who prefer a simple tot of meths or industrial ethanol for elevenses, sturdy, value-for-money drinking vessels in aluminium or stainless steel.

During the 1700s, wild habitats had become so depleted that huntsmen were reduced to chasing 'carted deer' – semi-tame animals brought to the intrepid sportsmen in a cart and released in front of them. Too valuable to be killed, the dogs were specially trained not to harm them. Those that gave a lively chase became stars in their own right. The most famous was a deer called 'Compton', renowned for his 'most determined courage and inexpressible speed'.

'Royal stags' have at least 12 points (or 'tines') to their antlers. In Scotland, a 'rack' of antlers placed over the hall door of a house or castle brings luck and safety to anyone who walks under it, provided it doesn't fall off.

In the UK, 35 million pheasants are reared and released onto shooting estates each year and 75,000 metric tonnes of lead shot are discharged into the countryside.

Anyone who has watched the All Blacks, the New Zealand rugby team, will have seen a *haka*, the traditional dance form of the Maori of New Zealand.

1. Stand with arms horizontal – right above left, knees slightly bent.

2. *Ka mate, ka mate!* Slap thighs twice. **3.** *ka ora!* Slap chest.

7. *puhuruhuru* Keep left fist pumping while moving right palm diagonally to the groin. **8.** *Nana nei i tiki mai whakawhiti te ra* Right fist pump, left fist pump, edging forwards.

Canoes

Performed to lay down a challenge to their opponents before a game, the haka has ancient origins, dating back to canoe-hauling chants and predates the Maori arrival in New Zealand in the 14th century.

There are many different types of haka: the one most often used by the New Zealand rugby team is called the *Ka Mate*. It was first regularly performed by the New Zealand team that visited Britain in 1905.

Sex

For a dance that is now used to put the fear of God into people, the words are more raunchy than intimidating, describing a young man's first nervous experience of sex. The full chant is known as the *Kikiki* (literally 'jabbering'). It begins *Kikiki kakaka kau ana! Kei waniwania taku tara* (Stuttering, shaking and naked! I'm brushed by your crotch) and goes on to describe the sexual act in graphic detail. The bit that the All Blacks now recite actually describes the inevitable 'climax':

Ka mate! Ka mate!
I am dying, I'm dead!
Ka ora! Ka ora!
No, I'm alive, fully alive!
Tenei te tangata puhuruhuru
A hairy (i.e. virile) man
Nana nei i tiki mai whakawhiti te ra!
who can bring joy and peace!
Upane, ka upane!
Together, side by side,
Whiti te ra!
we can make the sun shine!

Death

This chant was made famous by the legendary warrior, Te Rauparaha (c.1768-1849) of the Ng ti Toa tribe. He narrowly escaped death at the hands of his enemies by hiding in a sweet potato storage pit, while a friendly chief's wife sat over him. Terrified, her private parts inches from his face, he recited the end of the Kikiki to celebrate his release. From then on it became *'Te Rauparaha's Ka Mate'* and the Maori made up a sanitised translation to avoid shocking the prudish British settlers.

As a war dance the Kikiki haka made sense – conquering fear in battle was much like conquering fear in sex. Add to this the fact that the Maori often fought naked and an erection was seen as a mark of courage and you have a rather different angle on the haka: it's the ultimate sex and death anthem. Watching international rugby may never be the same again.

And now you can practise the Ka Mate haka at home using our 12 step how-to guide illustrated above.

PHOTOGRAPHY BY BRIAN RITCHIE

4. *ka ora!* Put hands in air. [REPEAT] **5.** *Tenei te* Right fist pump. **6.** *tangata* Left fist pump.

9. *A, upane!* Right fist upright, slap forearm twice. **10.** *ka upane!* Left fist upright, slap forearm twice.
11. *A, upane, ka upane, whiti te ra!* Slap right forearm once, then left forearm once.

12. *Hi!* Jump in the air.

Men only?

Traditionally women danced in the front ranks of the haka. The women who were given the most prominent positions were those most proficient in the art of *pukana* (rolling the eyes back in their head so only the whites were showing).

Hark the Heralds

The boast of heraldry, the pomp of pow'r'
Is quoted often, even to this very hour,
But few there are, these unbeknighted days
Who truly have an eye for heraldry's beknighted ways.
An eminent, if antiquated art
That surely brings noblesse to human heart.
Did I say 'antiquated'? Let me recant
For tis of now, as much as Dec and Ant;
With advertising message thrust at every hand
What is a coat of arms, if not a brand,
When Merrill Lynch's bull-emblazoned upstart
Will drive a Porsche, branded with the arms of Stuttgart?

Explaining both the artistry and charms,
Of what it really takes to make a coat of arms,
The age of chivalry, of warrior and of hero
Was on the whole enacted incognito;
For how on earth to recognise your armoured man
When decked from top to toe in metal can?
When clad in vambrace, beaver, cod and cuisse,
Hard to tell if master or, indeed, if miss;
Hard to tell if friend or fiendish foe
When all of you's obscured from head to tippy-toe.
But add to this a bar, a stripe or two,
Here a splash of red, there a little splash of blue,
A lion, a bird, a horse, a faithful hound,
A star, a bar, a square, a round,
A simple motif on an empty shield
And suddenly the faceless are revealed.
And knowing who's within th'anonymous armour
The field of joust or battle rings with cheery clamour:
'Yay, Sir Tom!' 'What ho, Sir Hugh!'
'Nice helm, Sir John, and how's the world with you?'

Oft from humble start the arts conspire
To flourish, blossom and inspire,
And heraldry, no less, became so rich an art
Requiring Heralds to sanction and impart,
Ensuring none but those of just or worthy cause
Bore upon them arms, upheld by laws.
And such an art and science then evolved
With content, colour, form and protocol resolved.

Yet straight away we come across a glitsch
Requiring us to scratch a dialectic itch;
For little more dismays the herald's breast
Than to call a coat-of-arms a 'crest'.
Where sits the crest itself? Above the whole,
An object or device from th' armorial roll,
Attached by knots to helm or helmet
And neatly tidied up by wreath or chaplet.
From whence is draped in tattered curls
The mantling, slashed and hacked in decorative swirls,
As if in battle ripped to shreds
Whilst keeping sun off armour-plated heads.
But gravity maintains its natural rights herein,
Requiring means to carry and to underpin.
Supporters, then, perform at left and right*
To give the shield the dignity of height,
And any man or beast with shoulders broad
With best foot forward can uphold the hoard,
Much as, of course, our queenly lion and unicorn,
An illustration of such burden nobly borne.

We digress. Within this knightly frame at last displays
The shield itself, in all its diverse, artful ways.
And schemes of colours, metals, shapes
and forms,
Beasts and objects, flora, fauna, stuff of copious tomes.
Animate, inanimate, florid, geometric,
Tinctures, chequers, furs and patterns diametric,
Rampant, statant, passant zoos
Abide within a wealth of hues,
And almost any object known to man
Is up for grabs within the rich armorial plan.

Horses, unsurprisingly, abound,
As does his master's favourite hound;
And hawks and horseshoes grace such a shield
Whose bearer maybe hunts thro' thicket and thro' field,
Where curls the bristly hedgehog in a ball;
The punning choice of Harrisons one and all
(For 'herisson', as every schoolboy knows,
Is French for 'hedgepig', down to his tiny toes,
Who, quaintly, in the herald's art
Is often known as 'urchin', bless his little heart).
Harts and hinds are oft entwined in chain
Against the which their rampant postures strain.
Many nobles favoured hands and hearts
Together with a slew of other body parts,
Along with savage heads and human figures
And bloody trophies from the crusades' rigours,
Whose prodding halberds, beat in armourer's forge,
Cry 'Prod for England, Harry and St. George!'
And herons, herrings, fish and fowl gymnastic
Swell the ranks of critturs more fantastic
(And oft unlikely bearing may prevail,
Such as the hauriant fish, who's standing on its tail).
The hippogriffs a truly awkward chump
Part lion, part eagle, bonded with a horse's rump
While hippocampus' altogether damper charms
Has pretty seahorse prominent on many arms.
But beware the harpy, fearful piece of crumpet,
Half-maid, half-vulture, wholly strumpet,
Whose female assets man must
never court
And, dare we say, we know
the very sort...

Domestic grief we'll quickly put aside
But take the quirky hurt within our stride;
A blueish disc, and somewhat strange to choose
That clearly represents a hurtful, purple bruise.
The list unfolds; there's more, and better,
And bear in mind we've only scoped one single
letter,
But time and place require a sense of closure
So just a couple more, at least, for our composure.

Tis true that 'music soothes the savage breast'
So here's the means to lay this piece to rest;
The frequent harp adorns the scutcheon's boast
To soothe the souls of many of the heavenly host,
Whose stars and angel wings contrive at every
hour
To mind us of our debts to higher power;
And therefore hatchments in the little country
church
Conclude our brief armorial search;
Funereal coats, whose marks of honour pay
A poignant homage to distinctions of an earlier day.
Noblesse may well oblige, but none's immune,
The final trump has all obliged to pay the piper's
tune.
For, when clogs are popped and soul takes wing

We'll harken then, to hear the herald angels sing.

WORDS BY DAVID COSTA

**A footnote here: I mentioned 'left and right'*
And should in truth have used the terms aright;
Sinister and dexter both apply,
but only from the bearer's eye;
With armorial feet stood firm upon
the ground
His left's your right,
and the other
way around.

FIVE HOLIDAY at HOME

***JULIAN** would like to be an actuary or an exotic dancer.*

***GEORGINA** likes to be called 'George' and is a bit of a tomboy.*

***ANNE** likes the sort of things girls like, but not girls like George.*

***DICK:** Likes cake – that's basically it.*

...and not forgetting Timmy the Dog!!

PHOTOGRAPHY BY JIM MARKS

With our carbon footprints hanging round our necks like a genocidal albatross why not take a leaf out of the Gang's book and save the planet by taking a holiday at home[1]? There's nothing the Costa Brava has that good old Blighty doesn't. So come on everybody, close your eyes and prepare for a treat...

Just look! Seaside resorts have been popular since Roman times although in Britain we were a bit backward, the idea only really catching on 2,000 years later. But since the mid-19th century[2] they've been something for all the family to look forward to – and you can see why.

Julian seems to have found a jolly nice place to stay. Plenty of fresh air and some colourful local graffiti. "The Safaitic language, a form of proto-Arabic found mainly in the Harrat Ash Shamah region which extends from southern Syria across Jordan and into northwestern Saudi Arabia, is only known from graffiti," he tells the others.

The gang, spoiled by years of indolent luxury now thankfully brought crashing down around their ears by the helpful activities of the banking sector, don't look too sure.

"But it was boarding houses very much like this that inspired Billy Butlin to create the first holiday camp[3]," enthuses Julian.

Nothing beats a relaxing morning on the sunny esplanade. “Wasn’t an esplanade originally an open area outside a fortress, cleared to provide an open field of fire against incoming attacks?[4]” asks Anne.

Looks like George can’t wait to get to the beach though. She’s such a tomboy!

What’s this? Dick’s off for a bracing dip. “Sea bathing”, he pants, “evolved from the 18th century craze for visiting mineral springs such as those in Spa in Belgium and was believed to cure disease – which is a load of homeopathic hokum as you all know.”

“See you later chaps…”

Wait Dick! Can’t you read the clearly displayed hazard signage. “In most countries an equilateral triangle signifies a hazard, although both border colour and width and background colours may vary from country to country,” comments Julian, sensibly.

“Bother”, chirrups Anne. “Looks like Dick has sunk into a colloidal hydrogel of sand and water[5]. Can I have his hat?” she adds hopefully.

“The density of quicksand means that the idea of actually completely sinking in is hooey, although the potential to become trapped might increase the risk from other hazards such as tide and exposure,” Julian points out.

“And besides, I saw Dick sneaking off to the pier.”

“Cop a load of this Timmy,” grins Dick, *What the Butler Saw*[6], invented by Herman Casler in 1894/5, utilised the flip-book animation principle, presenting and individually illuminating each of around 850 cards in order to give the effect of motion.”

“No Timmy. It’s horrid”, cries George.

Back on the beach it looks like the sun could come out any day now so the boys and girls decide to cool off with a proper swim in the sea.

Careful Anne, I can see your ankles. We don't want to inflame Dick do we?

What larks. The Gang are using their supple young bodies to form a flag semaphore message.

But what does it say? Sadly nothing, just like the cover of the Beatles album *Help!* which looks like it should spell HELP but actually spells NUJV[7].

George is off for a spot of sea fishing. Perhaps he'll catch a haddock (or offshore hake as it is sometimes known) or halibut or herring but not a houting[8].

Dick is a bit of an arenophile[9]. Sand has myriad uses. You can stand on it, sit on it, even write your name in it.

Dear me Dick, that's not right. You've written the German second person pronoun singular in the accusative.

Being blonde and fair-skinned, Anne applies a touch of sunblock to protect her from the fiery English sun.

"Russian fishermen on the Pacific coast buy Chinese Barbie dolls as bait, as they claim their blonde hair attracts herrings," laughs Anne.

Blondes really do have all the fun!

Time for a picnic. Looks like Anne's having a liquid lunch again.

And what's this? The Gang seem to have made a new friend! This donkey has his name on his harness, a tradition begun in the 19th century when the first holiday rides were offered on donkeys otherwise used in the shellfish-collecting industry.

Dick is having buns for lunch – with lashings of ginger beer[10] of course.

"Hefty horticulturist Gertrude Jekyll (1843-1932) had iced buns for breakfast every day[11]" he says, holding up two particularly fine examples.

After lunch Julian reads to Anne from his new book *Sodomy and the Pirate Tradition – English Sea Rovers in the Seventeenth-Century Caribbean* by B.R. Burg[12].

"As Burg says", quotes Julian, "The male engaging in homosexual activity aboard a pirate ship in the West Indies three centuries past was simply an ordinary member of his community, completely socialized and acculturated."

"Crikey!" Squeals George. "Look - a real pirate castle, albeit one with a poorly conceived hornwork[13] not conforming to the usual ground plan of the era. Perhaps a herisson[14] might improve the defensibility of the overall structure."

And look – a real pirate!

"Actually", drones Julian, "our archetypal image of a pirate is wholly wrong. Pirates didn't bury treasure, rarely sailed in galleons, didn't have hooks or eye-patches and only a couple had peg-legs. And there is no evidence that any owned a parrot.[15]

And, besides, he's wearing an M&S cardigan and that's Timmy on his shoulder."

"Arr" says the pirate rather unconvincingly, as the Gang adopt a pose eerily reminiscent of John Everett Millais' 1871 masterpiece *The Boyhood of Raleigh*.

"I'm actually flogging holidays in the Caribbean for a local travel agent, " says the pirate. "Did you know that a domestic dog has a bigger carbon footprint than a large car? So lose the dog and you can travel with a easy conscience – Arrr."

The Gang don't need to be told twice. Hispaniola[16] here we come!

"Bother!" says Timmy.

FOOTNOTES **1.** Not actually 'at home', as recommended in the 1942 Pathe newsreel which suggested staying in your home: 'The same sun shines on your garden or local swimming pools as at Tiddleypush-on-Sea.' **2.** British seaside holidays originate with wakes – religious festivals which, during the Industrial Revolution, were adapted into regular summer holidays in northern mill towns. Each area would nominate a 'Wakes Week' during which all the mills would close and fairs and trips to the seaside would be arranged. **3.** Billy Butlin (1899–1980) got the idea for his first seaside holiday camp whilst watching miserable families in Skegness cowering listlessly in the rain, as they were banned from returning to their boarding houses between mealtimes but had nowhere else to go. **4.** The term was actually first used in 1696 to describe the glacis of the counterscarp in a fortification, as Anne should jolly well know. **5.** Quicksand. **6.** More correctly Mutoscopes, 'What the Butler Saw' merely being the title of one of the more popular Mutoscope titles in England. **7.** The US version was slightly rearranged and spells NVUJ, which still doesn't make sense. **8.** The houting, a fish of the *Salmonidae* family once found in the UK, is now extinct. The last true houting was caught on the lower Rhine in 1940. **9.** An arenophile is someone who collects sand. Yes, really. **10.** As Dick and Anne well know, proper ginger beer is alcoholic (up to 11%) and is made using the Ginger Beer Plant, which is not a plant at all but a composite organism consisting of the yeast *Saccharomyces florentinus* and the bacterium *Lactobacillus hilgardii.* **11.** Along with sausages, eggs and coffee – according to a letter from Edwin Lutyens who visited her in August 1909. **12.** New York University Press, rev. edition (31 Jan 1995). **13.** A single-fronted outwork, the head of which consists of two demi-bastions connected by a curtain and joined to the main body of the work by two parallel wings. **14.** A barrier of stakes arranged on open ground in front of a fortification to prevent direct attack, from the French *hérisson* – hedgehog. **15.** For further details see *The Second Book of General Ignorance*, available now from all good bookshops. **16.** The formal name for the Caribbean island containing the sovereign states of the Dominican Republic and Haiti. When Columbus took possession of the island in 1492 he named it *La Isla Española*, meaning 'The Spanish Island'. The native Taino Amerindians called it Haití ('Mountainous Land').

Hermaphrodites

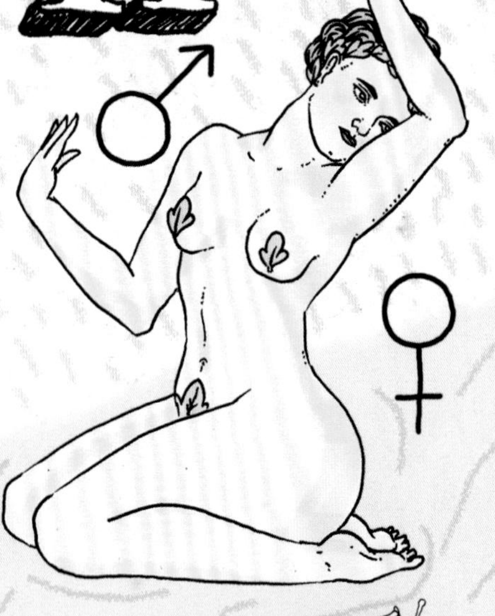

Hermaphroditus was a Greek god, son of Hermes and Aphrodite (this was, like, 'ages' ago). When he was 15, probably on his gap year, he went travelling through unknown lands and met a water nymph named Salmacis, who immediately fell in love with him. Strangely - considering he was a fifteen-year-old lad - he refused her erotic advances, and instead went for a dip in her pool. Seeing her chance, Salmacis grabbed hold of him, snogging away like a good 'un, and refused to let go. She cried out to the gods that she and Hermaphroditus should never be parted - and the gods granted her wish, albeit in their own typically unhelpful way. Hermaphroditus and Salmacis found their bodies merged together, into a creature that was both male and female.

In biology, a hermaphrodite is any organism that has both male and female organs. 'Protogynous' hermaphrodites start out female and become male; 'protoandrous' hermaphrodites start out male and become female; and 'simultaneous' hermaphrodites are both at once from the start.

Slugs & Snails

Land snails are simultaneous hermaphrodites. Their foreplay lasts for six hours. This involves much rubbing, biting and waggling their eyestalks at one another, after which they swap sperm. Banana slugs are also of the simultaneous persuasion. Their penises are located near their heads and are almost as long as their entire bodies. During mating, they insert these into each other, forming what looks very much like a yin and yang sign made of bananas. When they're done, one of them sometimes chews the other one's penis off, in an activity known as 'apophallation'. It's thought that this improves the mutilator's chances of passing on his genes, by increasing the number of females in the population. Occasionally, both slugs will de-penis each other - which must rather defeat the object.

Earthworms

Another simultaneous hermaphrodite, the earthworm, is ready for sex at four weeks old. While mating, worms enter a state in which they do not respond to light or touch – ah, what it is to be young! Once fertilised, the worms' clitella - the bulging rings round their middles - slip off over their heads, seal themselves at both ends, and become cocoons, from which tiny earthworms hatch.

Barnacles

Sex could be tricky for barnacles – who are also hermaphroditic – as they spend their entire adult lives glued to one spot. What makes it possible is having the largest penis-to-body ratio in the animal kingdom, enabling them to reach out to distant partners. "Crustacean, penis eight times longer than body, seeks similar. Object: romance and perpetuation of genes. GSOH. Not interested in long walks." Barnacles can change the shape and size of their organs-of-joy to suit circumstances. In rough water, they develop shorter, knobbier items, which don't wobble around in the current.

Clown Fish

Clownfish are protoandrous hermaphrodites. They live in groups with a hierarchy based on size. Females are larger than males and males are larger than non-breeding males. If the female dies, the most senior male changes sex and gets promoted to female, while the non-breeder below him/her moves up to breeder. Each fish politely keeps its body mass 20% smaller than its immediate superior. Amongst protogynous reef fish – where females get promoted by turning male – things are less easy-going. Fights can break out when the second-largest male has his ambitions of advancement thwarted. You can see his point; he's spent all this time as Number Two male, and now, suddenly, he's still Number Two, having been leapfrogged by an uppity transsexual.

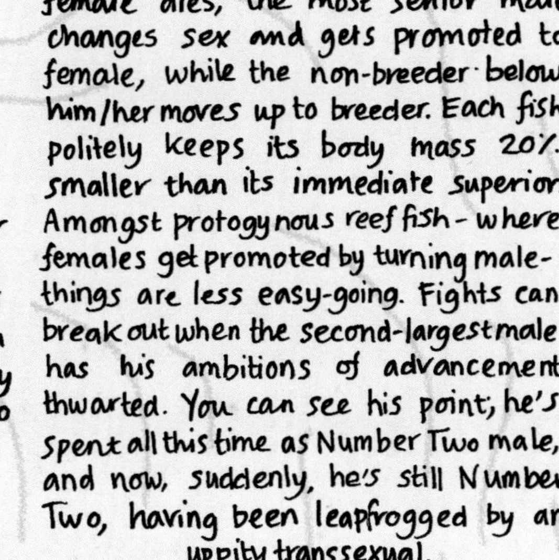

Comb Jelly

Another hermaphrodite, the Warty Comb Jelly, or Sea Walnut, tends towards self-reliance. When the time comes to reproduce, it disgorges from its mouth many thousands of eggs and sperm, which fertilize externally. A fascinating and breathtakingly beautiful creature, but not one you'd really want to kiss.

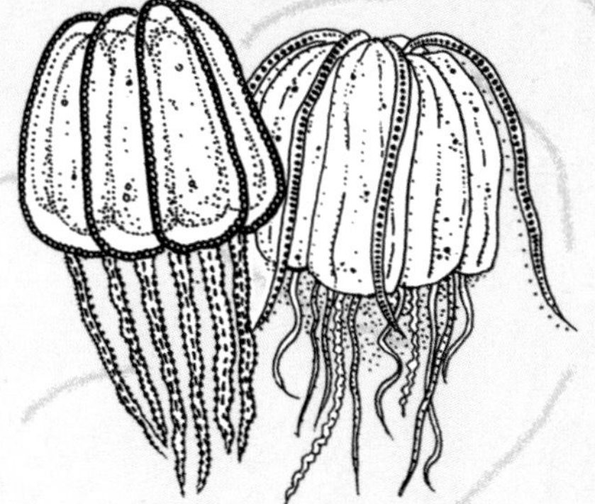

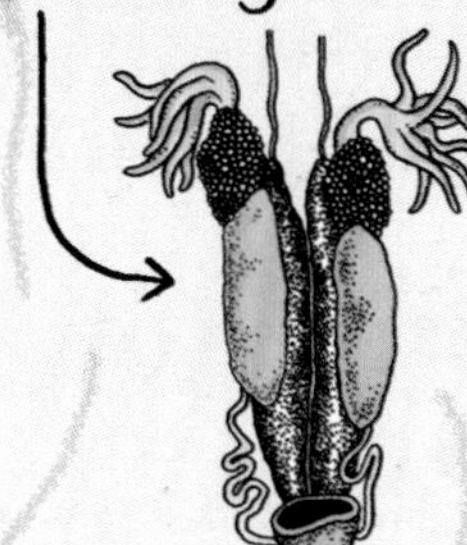

Cane Toad

Cane toads aren't hermaphrodites – but they're open to persuasion. If you castrate a cane toad (though we urge you to resist the temptation), a spherical, brownish object inside it will develop into fully functional ovaries. This object is called a Bidder's organ – named after lustrously bearded Latvian anatomist, Friedrich Bidder (1810–1894). Bidder's organ only develops in two situations. 1) If the male toad's genitals are not working properly but still intact. 2) if scientists remove them for experimental purposes. As a result, no one has any idea what the point of Bidder's organ might be.

Katie Scott

ARE YOU A HIPPOPOTAMUS?

Ten ways to tell

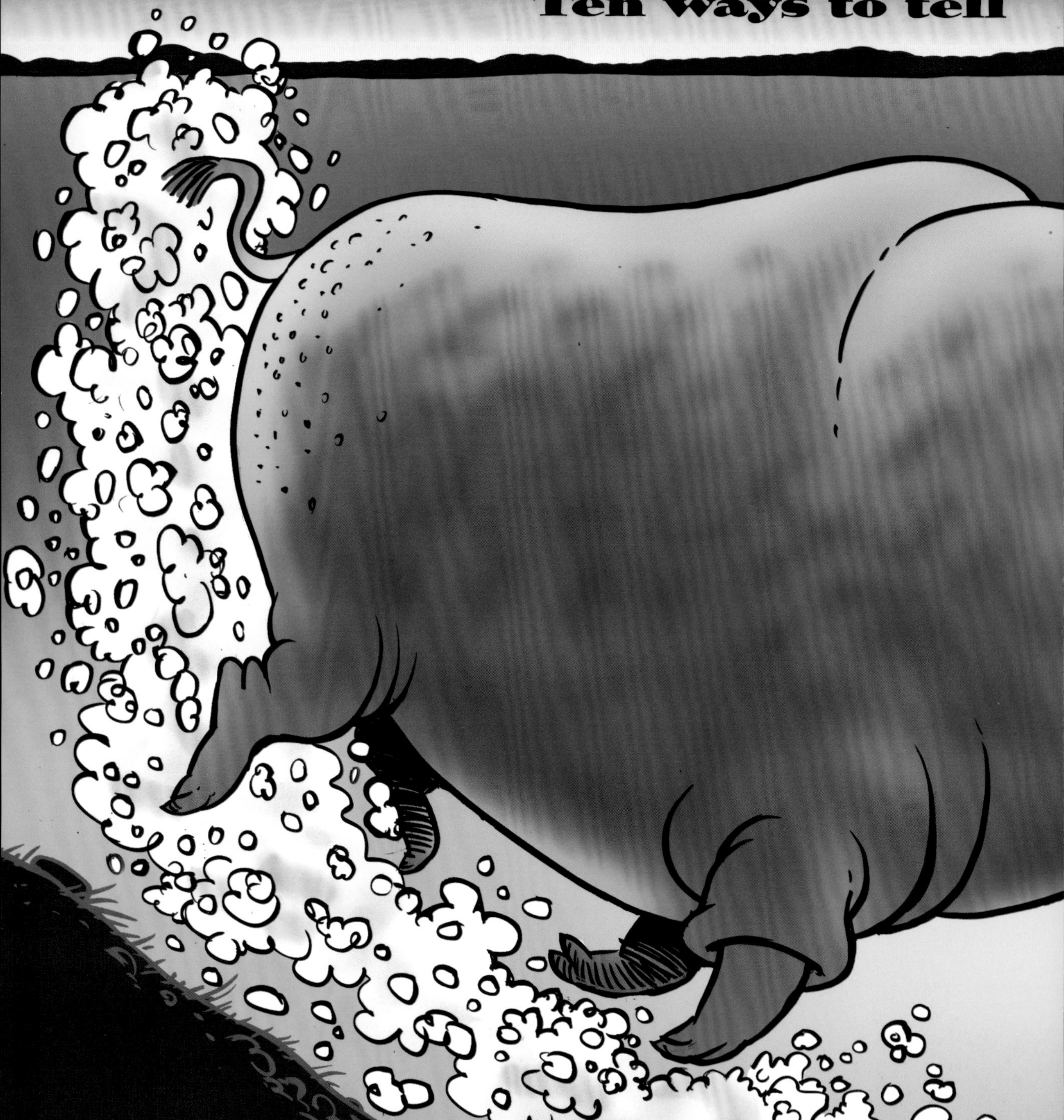

1. CAN YOU SWIM?

If so, you're not a hippo. Despite spending most of their lives in water, hippos don't swim. They can't even float. They trundle along the river bed, pointing their toes like ballet dancers. When they're asleep, an automatic reflex pushes their bodies off the bottom every five minutes or so, to surface for breath.

2. DOES ROLLING OVER & OVER IN WATER AID YOUR DIGESTION?

Bubbles are often observed breaking the surface as adult hippos roll over underwater – it's thought that the action helps them relieve their flatulence. Or they may just be trying to scratch their backs on the river bed. Young hippos, it's thought, simply roll for fun.

ARE YOU A HIPPOPOTAMUS? (MORE...)

3. ARE YOU FROM SUFFOLK?

One of the world's richest sources of hippo fossils is a 100,000-year-old site in Ipswich. Britain is thought to be the most northerly point hippos reached before the last ice age set in. More puzzling to archaeologists is the mass hippo grave in Cyprus, containing hundreds of charred hippo bones. They're dated 1,000 years earlier than the first known human habitation there. So who ate all the hippos?

4. ARE YOUR FEMALE RELATIVES A BIT ROUGH?

Fights between bull hippos are rarely fatal: they pack it in when they've worked out which one is stronger. The cows are a different matter. When they fancy claiming a choice piece of beach, they've been known to take it from the dominant bull by force – ignoring the Queensberry-style rules that govern the males, and attacking from behind in gangs.

5. DO YOU SWEAT SUNTAN LOTION?

Hippos are almost hairless, but never get sunburned. They exude a bright red substance known as 'blood sweat' (it's neither). This covers their skin in a layer of sun-screening mucus and contains an antibiotic called hipposudoric acid. Despite soaking in dirty water, hippos' wounds hardly ever become infected.

6. WOULD FRIENDS DESCRIBE YOU AS 'SKITTISH?'

For millions of years, hippos' ancestors were small, agile land-dwellers. They gradually evolved into huge, aquatic animals with no real predators – but their psychology hasn't caught up. They still behave like a vulnerable prey species, absurdly easily alarmed, and apt to become aggressive if they imagine themselves under threat.

7. DOES DUNG PLAY A LARGE PART IN YOUR LIFE?

The equivalent in hippo diplomacy of 'frank discussions' is the so-called 'dung shower'. When two male hippos meet, they park up bottom-to-bottom, defecating copiously and rapidly twirling their tails. Having thus coated his rival, each bull trots away, honour satisfied. A male wishing to join a herd signals his submission to the dominant bull's authority by lifting his rear end high out of the water and meekly letting his droppings plop out without any challenging tail action. Hippo calves nibble their dominant bull's dung. One rather far-fetched theory for this behaviour is that the dung contains chemicals from which they get genealogical information, telling them how they're related to the rest of the herd – a sort of 'Poo Do You Think You Are?'

8. NOT BEING FUNNY, BUT ARE YOU JUST A TOUCH TOWARDS THE OBSESSIVE END OF THE SPECTRUM?

When hippos leave the water at night to eat grass, they always enter and exit at precisely the same point. The resulting ruts, called 'gateways', can be 6' (1.82m) deep and are exactly one hippo wide. As the animals amble up the gateway to their 'lawn', they place their feet in the same grooves. Year after year, there will be not even the slightest variation.

9. ARE YOU INVISIBLE?

Though huge and gregarious, hippos are amongst the least-studied, most mysterious land mammals – mainly because they spend up to 20 hours a day largely inactive, in water made opaque by them stirring up the silt. All that can be seen of them is eyes, ears and nostrils. When they are ashore, it's either dark, or they're asleep.

10. DO YOU HAVE A LARGE VOCABULARY AND A LOUD VOICE?

(That doesn't necessarily make you a hippo, of course; you could be a QI panellist.) Hippos are chatty in the water, but silent on land. The bulls' 'wheeze-honk' is one of Africa's loudest noises, and is usually replied to by the entire herd in chorus. But it has recently been discovered that 80% of hippo communication takes place underwater, via large blobs of blubber under their jaws, and is far more complex than previously thought. That explains why we know so little about their social organisation – it's conducted inaudibly to our ears, as well as invisibly to our eyes.

Glen Baxter

Nº 129 FINDING A USE FOR POLENTA

Nº 249 ONLY EVER PURCHASE SEMTEX FROM A REPUTABLE DEALER

Nº 286A BRIGHTEN UP YOUR HOME!

KNIT YOUR OWN NUCLEAR SUBMARINE

Nº 329 HOW TO RID YOUR HOME OF UNWANTED PESTS

ho!ho!

'... and just where *have* you been hiding all my life?'

'Alaska.'

'You see, Huntsucker, it's all part of the sickness of the age.'

'Why don't you grow up?'

'... I told you these SatNavs couldn't be trusted didn't I Stan, didn't I?'

'... why not look at it this way, Crawley, your job is your bonus'

'Shouting? SHOUTING? I'll tell you why I'm SHOUTING! Because I'm wrong, that's why I'm SHOUTING!'

'It's filthy, it's sexual, it's violent, it's sick, it's perfect.'

'... oh he's always into something new, is our George.'

'Before we commence this long, in-depth interview, errm, may I ask if you've ever considered changing your name, Mr Slack Scrotum?'

Too wet to woo.

Hello, Half-fans!

A half-hearted welcome to our page of two halves to each and every other one of you. If you're looking for half-truths and demi-facts (and studies show that 50% of us are), then read on – you're already halfway there.

According to the nursery rhyme, the Grand Old Duke of York was a man who liked to do things by halves. But who was this halfwit, and why, in the name of all that's semi-sensible, did he park 10,000 men halfway up a hill in such a lamentable state of neither-up-nor-downness? There are several theories. Maybe he was the Duke of York who was killed in 1460 (halfway through the Wars of the Roses) when he made a half-hearted attack on a big Lancastrian army half-way down the hill outside his castle and ended up with his head on a spike. Or maybe the nursery rhyme is about Prince Frederick, the Duke of York who went off half-cocked and lost a battle against the army of that well-known half-pint, Napoleon, in 1794. The fact is, nobody really knows, and I have half a mind to think it might just be a nursery rhyme.

HARVEY HALFWAY'S

People often ask me: 'Harvey – why, in the name of all that's half-priced, do you insist on flying the Stars and Stripes halfway up the flagpole at Halfway House? Everybody knows you're half-English, half-Scottish, and half-Welsh, not American.' The answer is that if we want to fly our flag at half-mast (which we jolly well do), then Old Glory is the only flag which is officially half-masted halfway up the flagpole. All other nations call it 'half-mast' but actually fly the flag two-thirds of the way up, the frauds. And I'm sorry, but that kind of thing doesn't half give me the pip.

According to Melvyn Bragg, half-time at football was invented in the days when all football was played between different schools, each of which had their own rules, so that they could play according to one school's rules in the first half and the other school's in the second half. That sounded like a pretty half-baked theory to us, so we checked with the FA...

In England a 'half-and-half' is a mixture of two types of beer. In Scotland, it's a whisky with a beer chaser. But if you want to get half-cut, don't ask for a half-and-half in America; over there it's a mixture of half milk and half cream, and they put it in their coffee.

...Their historian went and rootled about in the archives for half an hour and then said he doesn't think it's true: according to him, half-time has always been so that teams could change ends in case there was a slope or a wind blowing from one end of the pitch to the other – and that was the custom even when both teams came from the same school. Too clever by half, Melvyn!

Scandinavian shoe thieves have come up with a cunning plan for stealing expensive shoes, half-a-pair at a time. In Malmö, Sweden, there are 125 shoe shops, and they all put the left shoes on display and keep the right shoes in the stockroom, reasoning that nobody would want to steal piles of lefties without the righties to go with them. Even so, the display shoes keep going missing, and no one could work out why ... until they realised that just over the border, in Denmark, the shoe shops have the opposite custom: they put the righties on display and keep the lefties in the store-room. The cunning Swedish shoe-sharpers just smuggle their half-pairs over the border and then half-inch the other halves from a shop in Copenhagen.

Here at Halfway House we like to do things by halves, but only about 50% of the time. The rest of the time we do just the opposite! So now it's time to hand over to my better half, Henrietta, for the other half of our page of two halves.

Helloooo! Henrietta Halfway here...

PAGE OF 2 HALVES

During the Second World War, cow carcasses imported for meat were folded in half to save space in the holds of cargo ships (they took the bones out first. Duhhh...). Each carcass was folded over once - but how many times can you fold a piece of paper in half? Seven, right? Wrong! Not even half-right! That old myth was knocked on the head by American student Britney Gallivan in 2001. She worked out a clever equation and then tested it by getting a piece of lavatory paper half-a-mile or 800m long (maybe not quite - but jolly long, anyway) and folding it in half twelve times. Here's the interesting thing, though: if you could fold a piece of paper in half indefinitely, it would double in thickness each time – and if you folded it 51 times its thickness would equal the distance from the Earth to the Sun!

Last year Harvey decided he wanted to race his horse (a half-bred hunter, naturally) in a point-to-point. To his perverse satisfaction, he fell off halfway round the course, because he had been cunningly half-lengthed by one of the other riders. Half-lengthing is a trick the old pros play on inexperienced riders, and here's how it works: you gallop up to a jump alongside the other rider, then get your horse half-a-length ahead just before take-off. As your horse launches itself into the air you shout 'HUP!' at the top of your voice and hopefully this tricks the beginner's horse into jumping too early and landing right on top of the hedge. Hilarious! And it certainly made Harvey look like a halfwit.

Harvey is a delight to live with - a man, as I often say, for whom the glass is always half-full. Oddly enough, that's not because he's an optimist, or even because he's keen on halves; it's just that I keep filling it up, but he's a frightful dipsomaniac.

I don't know about you, but I seem to spend half my life slaving over a lukewarm stove. Today I found I didn't have half the ingredients I needed for Harvey's breakfast, but half a loaf is better than no bread (actually, in my view half a loaf is better than a whole loaf – but that may just be me). Similarly, a cake is better than a biscuit. 'Why in the name of half-measures is that?' you may be half-inclined to ask. Well, the word 'biscuit' comes from the Latin *bis coctus*, which means 'twice-baked'. Biscuits were originally cakes which had been baked a second time to dry them out and preserve them – so a cake is nothing but a half-baked biscuit. Yum!

You know how you can cut an earthworm in half and get two worms? Well, actually, you can't! Sometimes the head end survives, if you haven't cut off too much of the tail – but the tail can't survive on its own. That's just a story you half-remember from when you were small which they forgot to put you right on after you grew up.

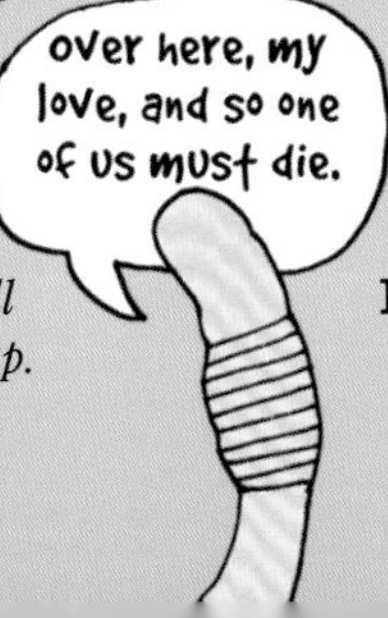

That's all we've got room for on our page of two halves. We could easily have written half as much again! Cheerio, half-fans – and keep it half-sized! Your pals,

Harvey and
Henrietta Halfway

MORE
Horsefeathers
They used to have terrible trouble with people getting TB from ice cream.
Was that because they were making it out of badgers?
Not all of it. But the most popular flavour was badger.
A humming bird's heart beats a thousand times a minute but it can slow down to fifty beats a minute when . . .
When it sees a policeman.
You truly are a Renaissance man.
Well ... I wear tights, put it that way.
Did you know that Members of Parliament never shake hands with each other?
They just go straight in for a head butt.
Since when do fish have tongues? And why?
How else are they going to whistle?
Looting and pillaging? What is pillaging?
It's kind of sacking, ransacking, stealing from, pilfering and taking things, burgling, taking ... pillaging.
So – the same as looting.

What's the best way to weigh your own head?
I would weigh myself, then go to the swimming baths and bob and get people to feed me 'til I sank. Then come back out and weigh myself again.
Yes, that sounds scientific.
What's the trick to walking over hot coals?
Wear shoes?
What starts with H and means you'll always be the bridesmaid and never the bride?
Hepatitis C.
You're close.
Herpes then.
The human brain is the most complex thing we know of in the universe.
Have you ever filled in a VAT return?
VAT
A pipe confers a kind of respectability I think.
Not if it has a lump of crack in it.
We're very grateful to Steve Colgan, the artist responsible for these pictures.
I'm not grateful to him.
I'm with Alan. I'm not grateful at all.
We might do a picture of Steve later, see how he likes it.

PISSHEAD MCWHURTLE, THE WILD MAN OF EASTBOURNE

Well, there's two kinds of Hell's Angel, the ones with wings and the ones with tyres. So let's leave aside the mean ass dudes on mean ass machines for a moment and consider instead those magnificent men in their flying machines, and the Howard Hughes film that first burned the name Hell's Angels into the popular subconscious.

Howard Hughes

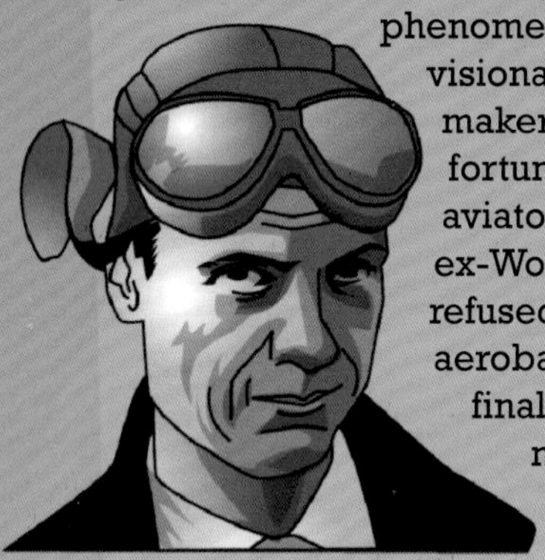

Hughes, in addition to being a golfing phenomenon, maths whizz, visionary inventor, film-maker and heir to a fortune, was a pioneer aviator. When his crew of ex-World War 1 stunt pilots refused to attempt the aerobatics required for the final scene of Hughes' movie *Hell's Angels*, Hughes himself piloted the plane which made the final edit - even if the plane itself ended up as a pile of matchsticks. Despite their relative caution, three aviators and a mechanic didn't survive to make the first-night screening at Grauman's Chinese Theater in Hollywood on May 24th 1930.

Harlow

Star of *Hell's Angels* and a Hughes protégé, Jean Harlow shot to fame as a peroxide *femme fatale.* Her acting skills were lambasted by the critics but as *Variety* stated: **'It doesn't matter what degree of talent she possesses ... nobody ever starved possessing what she's got.'** She it was who made the mistake of addressing Margot Asquith thus, **'Say - aren't you Margot Asquith?' to which Asquith witheringly replied, 'Yes dear, but the "t" is silent as in Harlow.'**

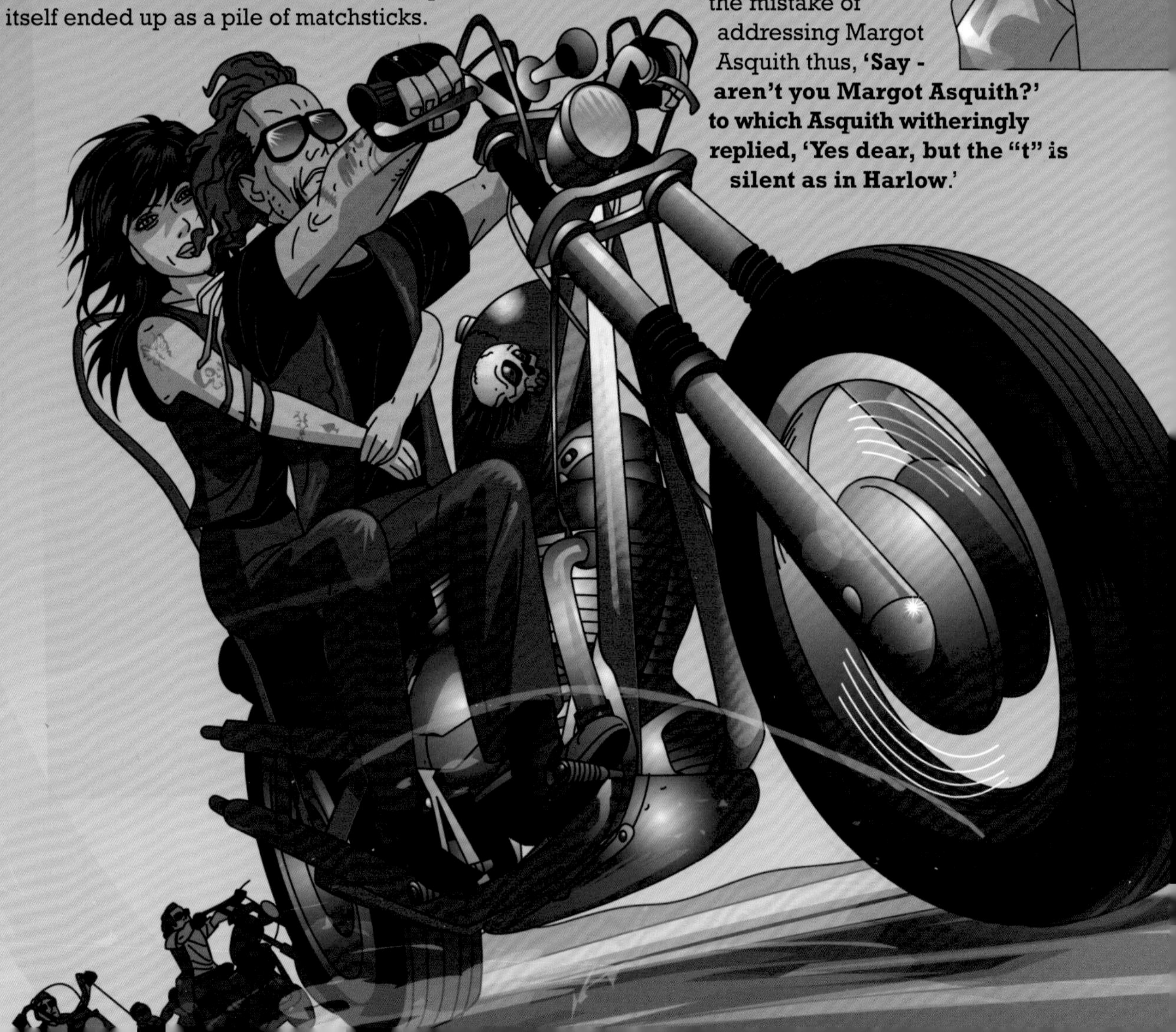

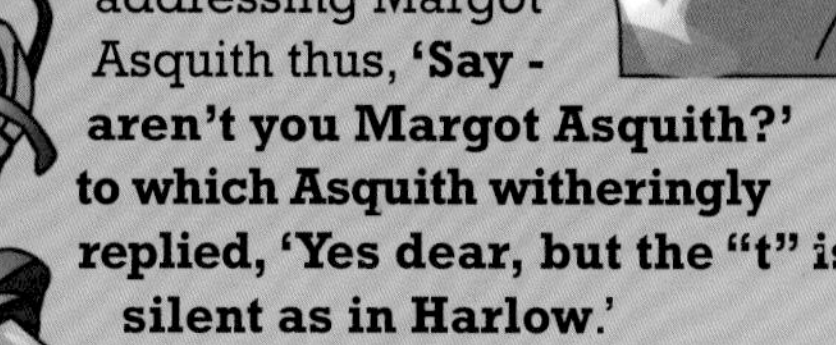

Hollister

World War 2 US bomber crews liberally adorned their B-52s and their flight leather jackets with a variety of edgy iconography including likenesses of Ms Harlow and the legend 'Hell's Angels'. It was men such as these - returning from the adrenalin buzz of aerial combat who needed something more than a nine-to-five job and a house with a picket fence - that first started tooling around with bikes and forming biker clubs. The favoured location for a lot of bikers was the West Coast and on July 4th 1947 the sleepy little town of Hollister was transformed into a drag strip as several thousand Hell Raisin' Bikers tore up and down the main street.

Hoodlums and Homosexuals

Pictures of the ensuing fracas made it to the pages of *Life* magazine. With reports that members of The Boozefighters Club lived up to their name, and with a tally of 50 arrests and 60 injuries, the California Attorney General, Thomas C. Lynch, fulminated about hoodlum biker gangs whose **'record of rape and violence, sex offences and homosexuality poses a threat to all of California'**. So middle America quaked whilst the Hollywood moguls dreamed.

Hollywood

In 1953 *The Wild One* seared its way across cinema screens, with Marlon Brando as Johnny, leader of a band of 'Hoodlum bikers' who wore the legend BRMC emblazoned across their leather jackets. BRMC as in Black Rebel Motorcycle Club.

'Hey Johnny, what are you rebelling against?' asked one of the juke joint gals.
'What you got?' Brando replied.

Middle America had another little shiver of apprehension as the nation's youth decided that they wanted a piece of the action for themselves.

Brando may no longer be with us but BRMC are still packing out stadiums.

Harley Davidson

A mean ass machine powerful enough to haul a truck and the bike most favoured by those West Coast biker gangs cruisin' the freeways. They'd learned to field strip their machines and build them up again in a style distinctly their own. Even though there are cheaper equivalents, there is nothing that quite matches the sheer sex on wheels appeal of a Harley.

Hunter S. Thompson

American iconoclast and documenter of the counter-culture, Thompson's mantra was, **'I hate to advocate drugs, alcohol, violence or insanity to anyone, but they've always worked for me.'** Documented his experiences of living with the Hell's Angels, got beaten up when he refused to cut them in for a share of the profits, and published the book that launched his career as a writer - *Hell's Angels: The Strange and Terrible Saga of the Motorcycle Gangs* in 1966.

Hell's Angels

When the name appears on the patch on their jackets it appears minus the apostrophe. For all other purposes the apostrophe remains. The patch belongs to the club not to individual members. Their primary motto is: ***'When we do right nobody remembers, when we do wrong nobody forgets.'***

Notorious as the kind of guys you don't want to mess with and the embodiment of your worst nightmare if you do, they are pre-eminent amongst the 'one percenter' motorbike clans. 'One percenter' refers to the American Motorbike Association's claim, in the wake of the 1947 Hollister fracas, that 99% of motorcyclists are law-abiding citizens and the remaining 1% are outlaws.

Hopper

Dennis Hopper, Hollywood bad boy and the man who created *Easy Rider*, hauling in his acting buddy Peter Fonda and Terry Southern as co-creatives. Hopper and Fonda had already made previous biker films, most notably Fonda's portrayal of Hell's Angel leader Heavenly Blues in the 1966 Roger Corman bike flick *The Wild Angels* which critic Leonard Maltin described as being 'Okay after 24 beers'. Heavenly Blues' eulogy at a fellow biker's funeral has since attained iconic status after being sampled by Primal Scream as part of the intro to *Loaded*.

'We want to be free! We want to be free to do what we want to do! We want to be free to ride. And we want to be free to ride our machines without being hassled by The Man. And we want to get loaded. And we want to have a good time! And that's what we're gonna do. We're gonna have a good time. We're gonna have a party!'

Easy Rider was an infinitely hipper film than any previous biker film, winning the Cannes Film Festival in 1969 and securing Hopper an Oscar for his directorial debut. A year later he was back to Bad Boy status, having gulled the suits at Universal to bankroll him as director, writer and star in the aptly titled (for Hopper) *Last Movie*. Listed in a book called *The Fifty Worst Films Of All Time*, the film failed to recoup the $1,000,000 that the old guys at Universal had advanced Hopper and he was a virtual pariah in Hollywood for much of the next 10 years, until Francis Ford Coppola cast him as a hypermanic Vietnam journalist in the 1979 blockbuster *Apocalypse Now*.

Hogs and Heifers

This is the name of a bar in the meatpacking district of Manhattan, that takes the confrontational ethos of bikerdom as its mantra. Unwary visitors are lambasted by barmaids equipped with loud hailers for ***'taking up valuable floor space, standing like a jackass when you should be buying a drink.'*** If you have a cast-iron will and are not suffering from major issues of self-worth then stick around and get slowly trolleyed, as you watch the barmaids abuse their clientele while dancing on the bar counter – a practice pioneered by owner Michelle Dell when she started work as a barmaid in the freezing winter of 1992 and it was the only way to keep warm. Nowadays the bar is fuller and warmer but the countertop clogging continues.

If however you are of a more delicate mindset then settle back with a beer from the fridge (much less frightening than the girls with tattoos, loud hailers and degrees in psychology), and watch *Coyote Ugly*, a film inspired by this notorious bar which now occupies locations in Manhattan and Las Vegas.

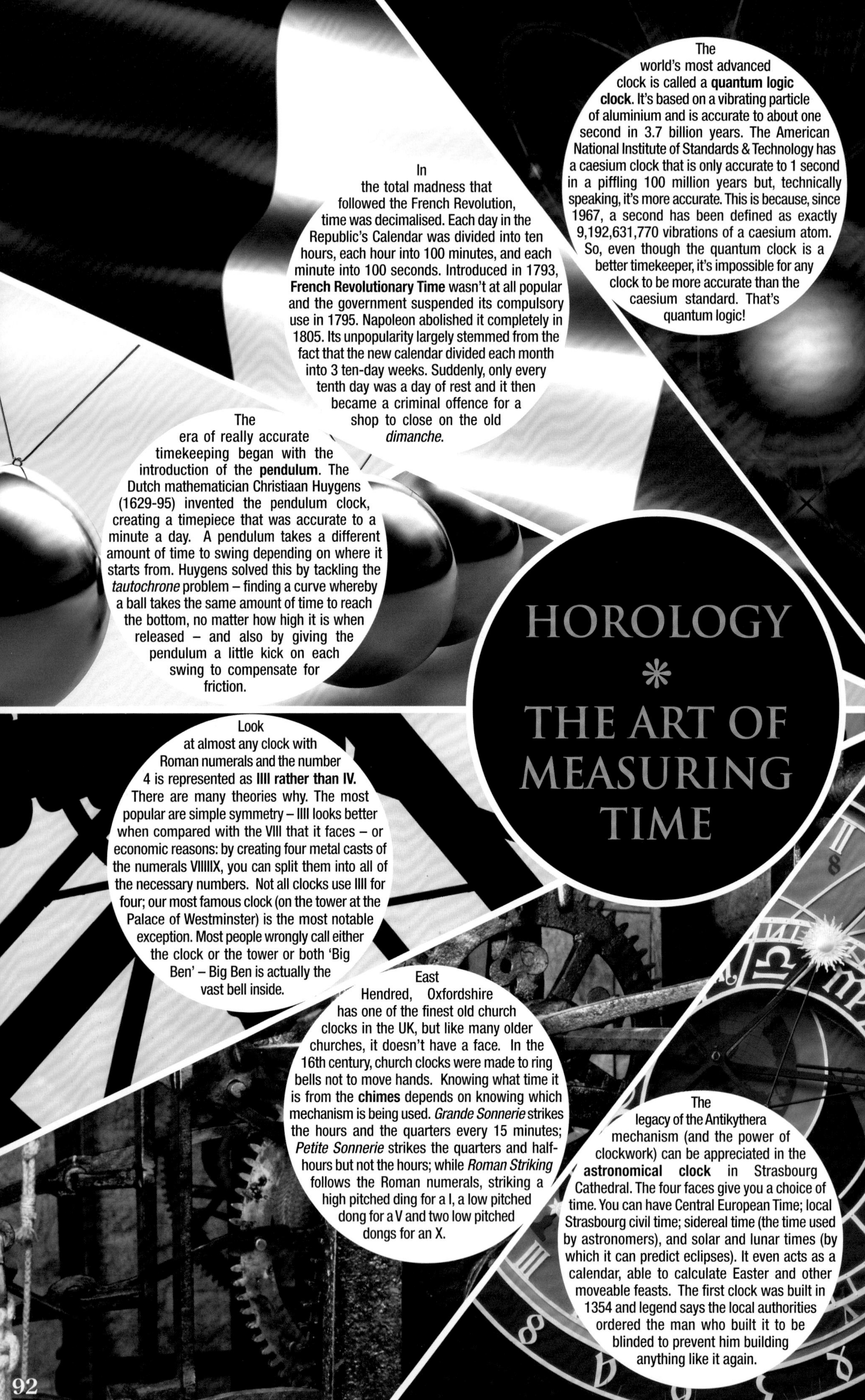

The world's most advanced clock is called a **quantum logic clock**. It's based on a vibrating particle of aluminium and is accurate to about one second in 3.7 billion years. The American National Institute of Standards & Technology has a caesium clock that is only accurate to 1 second in a piffling 100 million years but, technically speaking, it's more accurate. This is because, since 1967, a second has been defined as exactly 9,192,631,770 vibrations of a caesium atom. So, even though the quantum clock is a better timekeeper, it's impossible for any clock to be more accurate than the caesium standard. That's quantum logic!

In the total madness that followed the French Revolution, time was decimalised. Each day in the Republic's Calendar was divided into ten hours, each hour into 100 minutes, and each minute into 100 seconds. Introduced in 1793, **French Revolutionary Time** wasn't at all popular and the government suspended its compulsory use in 1795. Napoleon abolished it completely in 1805. Its unpopularity largely stemmed from the fact that the new calendar divided each month into 3 ten-day weeks. Suddenly, only every tenth day was a day of rest and it then became a criminal offence for a shop to close on the old *dimanche*.

The era of really accurate timekeeping began with the introduction of the **pendulum**. The Dutch mathematician Christiaan Huygens (1629-95) invented the pendulum clock, creating a timepiece that was accurate to a minute a day. A pendulum takes a different amount of time to swing depending on where it starts from. Huygens solved this by tackling the *tautochrone* problem – finding a curve whereby a ball takes the same amount of time to reach the bottom, no matter how high it is when released – and also by giving the pendulum a little kick on each swing to compensate for friction.

HOROLOGY * THE ART OF MEASURING TIME

Look at almost any clock with Roman numerals and the number 4 is represented as **IIII rather than IV.** There are many theories why. The most popular are simple symmetry – IIII looks better when compared with the VIII that it faces – or economic reasons: by creating four metal casts of the numerals VIIIIIX, you can split them into all of the necessary numbers. Not all clocks use IIII for four; our most famous clock (on the tower at the Palace of Westminster) is the most notable exception. Most people wrongly call either the clock or the tower or both 'Big Ben' – Big Ben is actually the vast bell inside.

East Hendred, Oxfordshire has one of the finest old church clocks in the UK, but like many older churches, it doesn't have a face. In the 16th century, church clocks were made to ring bells not to move hands. Knowing what time it is from the **chimes** depends on knowing which mechanism is being used. *Grande Sonnerie* strikes the hours and the quarters every 15 minutes; *Petite Sonnerie* strikes the quarters and half-hours but not the hours; while *Roman Striking* follows the Roman numerals, striking a high pitched ding for a I, a low pitched dong for a V and two low pitched dongs for an X.

The legacy of the Antikythera mechanism (and the power of clockwork) can be appreciated in the **astronomical clock** in Strasbourg Cathedral. The four faces give you a choice of time. You can have Central European Time; local Strasbourg civil time; sidereal time (the time used by astronomers), and solar and lunar times (by which it can predict eclipses). It even acts as a calendar, able to calculate Easter and other moveable feasts. The first clock was built in 1354 and legend says the local authorities ordered the man who built it to be blinded to prevent him building anything like it again.

The oldest known **sundials** are ancient Egyptian and Babylonian obelisks erected more than 5,000 years ago. Despite their antiquity, sundials are surprisingly versatile: there have been indoor sundials that use mirrors to reflect the sun; night-time moondials; and even a sundial alarm clock that used a magnifying glass to focus the sun's rays to ignite the gunpowder in a miniature cannon and fire it at a set time. The part of a sundial that casts the shadow is called a *gnomon.* Rare 19th-century pocket sundials put the gnomon onto a compass.

The Greek for the pedestal of a sundial (and hence the sundial itself) is ***analemma***, meaning a prop or support. Due to the Earth's tilt, and the fact that its orbit is not perfectly circular, the Sun is not at the same position in the sky at the same time every day, but follows a figure-of-eight path through the year. This path is also known as the analemma, and it explains why sundials are not always perfectly accurate. The average, or 'mean', position of the sun in the sky over the course of one year gives us the word 'mean' in the phrase 'Greenwich Mean Time'.

The **Prime Meridian** is an imaginary line of longitude that divides the world into Eastern and Western hemispheres. By international convention, this runs through the Royal Observatory in Greenwich, London where it is marked by a metal strip. In the church of Saint-Sulpice in Paris, there is a brass line set into the floor and running up an obelisk. At noon, the sun shines through a lens in a window and strikes the line at a different point on each day of the year. Despite whatever *The Da Vinci Code* says, it is not, and never has been, a prime meridian.

THE GODS CONFOUND THE MAN WHO FIRST FOUND OUT HOW TO DISTINGUISH HOURS.
CONFOUND HIM, TOO, WHO IN THIS PLACE SET UP A SUNDIAL,
TO CUT AND HACK MY DAYS SO WRETCHEDLY INTO SMALL PIECES!

TITUS MACCIUS PLAUTUS
(250-185 BC)

Sunset Mirage. The sun isn't always quite where you think it is. Light from the setting sun passes through a lot of atmosphere and the change in air density causes the light to bend (as when you look at your feet dangling in a swimming pool). It's for this reason, at the end of the day, that the sun appears to be higher in the sky than it actually is – an effect called a *superior mirage.* In fact, when you see the lower edge of the sun touch the horizon, the whole thing has actually already fallen completely below it.

In ancient India, the *Ghati* or *kapala* was used to measure time. This was a **copper bowl** with a hole in its bottom that floated in a basin of water and sank after one *nadika* (24 minutes, or 1/60th of a day). The great Islamic inventor Al Jazari (1136-1206) incorporated this mechanism into his fantastical 20-foot tall elephant clock. In another machine, Al Jazari used **ball bearings** set into a wax **candle**. These were released as it burned down, powering a dial that displayed the time. The Chinese were able to tell what time it was by **smell:** they had clocks in which burning joss sticks changed their fragrance at regular intervals.

The **Antikythera Mechanism** was discovered in a wreck under the Aegean Sea in 1900 but it was decades before anyone understood what it was. Built in about 100 BC and consisting of 72 superbly engineered geared wheels, it was able to determine the course of the sun, moon and known planets. It split the year into 365 days, making allowances for a leap every fourth year. It is the world's first analogue computer. Its discovery was said to be like opening Tutankhamun's tomb to find the decayed parts of an internal combustion engine; it is more valuable than the Mona Lisa.

H-Quiz

The answers

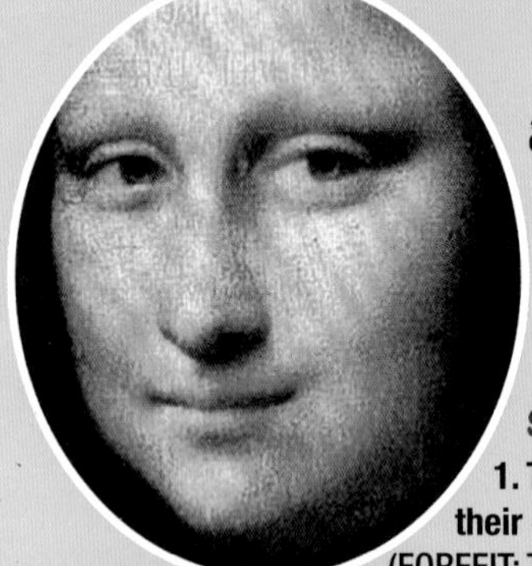

BIOLOGICAL SCIENCES

1. They don't have eyebrows/hair on their eyebrows. (2 points)
(FORFEIT: THEY'RE HORSE-FACED. MINUS 2)

2. Harrods. (2 points) It is thought all the hedgehogs on the island are descended from a pair bought at the department store in 1958.
(FORFEIT: HERM*. MINUS 2)
**Herm is the nearest Channel Island to Alderney. Smart answer but wrong.*

3. Hirudinea. (2 points) Leeches belong to the subclass *Hirudinea* of the phylum *Annelida* (segmented worms). Britain's only leech farm, Biopharm Ltd nr Swansea, a subsidiary of the Princess of Wales Hospital in Bridgend, sells 20,000 medicinal leeches a year at c. £10 each, all over Europe. It states that leeches have 32 brains, though technically this is one central brain with 32 separate clumps of ganglia (nerve cells containing motor neurons) controlling each segment.

4. Honeyguides. (2 points) Honeyguides are unique amongst birds in that they like eating wax. The Greater and Lesser Honeyguides survive on nothing but wax for up to 30 days. They are boring-looking brown birds from Africa that get their name from their bizarre habit of guiding people and other large mammals to bees' nests.

5. None. (2 points) The 34 muscles that bend the fingers are all in the palm and the mid forearm, connected to the finger bones by tendons, which move the fingers like marionettes. 17 of these muscles are in the palm, 18 in the forearm.

6. Either Honey Possum (2 points) **or Chinese Hamster** (2 points).
(FORFEIT: BLUE WHALE. MINUS 2)

7. The human ear. (2 points) The smallest bone is the stirrup bone, and the smallest muscles are the *stapedius* and the *tensor tympani*.

8. Hummingbirds. (2 points) The word for 'hummingbirdlike' is *trochilidine*. Hummingbirds are the only birds that can fly backwards or hover in still air. The system by which they fly is as different from that of other birds as a helicopter is from an aircraft. Giant Hummingbirds are so-called because they weigh three-quarters of an ounce (21g).

PPE (PHILOSOPHY, POLITICS & ECONOMICS)

1. Socrates. (2 points) His famously tricky wife was called Xantippe (from the Greek *xanthos*, 'yellow' or 'blonde', and *hippos*, 'horse').

> *'By all means marry: if you get a good wife you'll be happy, if you get a bad one you'll become a philosopher.'* SOCRATES

2. Household management. (2 points) From the Greek *oikos* (house) and *nomos* (law), from the verb *nemo* (to manage). The phrase 'home economics' is not pretentious, but it is tautologous.

3. St Helens South. (2 points) Represented, since 2001, by Shaun Woodward, married to Camilla Sainsbury, the supermarket heiress.

4. Heidegger. (2 points) Martin Heidegger (1889-1976) was the son of a village sexton. His magnum 1927 opus is *Sein und Zeit* ('Being and Time'). He was a member of the Nazi party 1933-1945.

5. His house, or his second home. (2 points) Parliamentary officials rejected his claim for the infamous duck house at source. A fees officer scrawled 'not allowable' next to the duckhouse claim.
(FORFEIT: DUCK, DUCKHOUSE MINUS 2)

6. Honduras. (2 points) 100 centavos = 1 lempira; 19 lempiras = 1 dollar. The Lempira replaced the peso in 1931. Named after the Lenca Indian resistance leader *Lempira* (1497-1537), who united 200 rival tribes against the Spanish and whose picture is on the 1 Lempira note.

7. Samuel Pepys. (2 points) Pepys (1633-1703) was Chief Secretary to the Admiralty (from 1673) under Charles II and James II. Famous for his diary, he was also an MP and a talented administrator. Although he had no naval experience, he reformed naval finances. He was also a fellow of the Royal Society. The title page of Newton's *Principia Mathematica* (published by the Royal Society) bears Pepys's name.

8. *'Here men from the planet earth first set foot upon the moon in July 1969. We came in peace for all mankind'* (2 points). These are the words on the plaque left behind on the moon by the first men to walk on it, Neil Armstrong and Buzz Aldrin, in 1969.

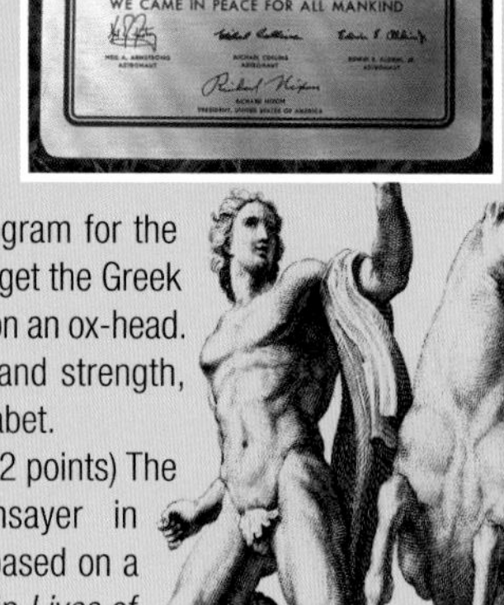

MODS & GREATS (CLASSICS TO YOU & ME)

1. Alexander the Great. (2 points) His horse was called Bucephalus (Ox-Head). The pictogram for the Phoenician aleph, from which we get the Greek alpha and the Roman A, is based on an ox-head. The ox was a symbol of power and strength, hence it's the 'leader' of the alphabet.

2. Beware the Ides of March. (2 points) The fatal prediction of the soothsayer in Shakespeare's *Julius Caesar* is based on a real event reported by Suetonius in *Lives of the Caesars*, written in about 110 AD. Spurinna was the most famous Etruscan haruspex (one who divines by entrails) of his time, but Caesar laughed off his prediction and entered the Senate on the day calling him a fraud - because the Ides of March had come, but he was still unharmed. Spurinna replied ominously that they had indeed come, but they had not gone…

3. Herod the Great. (2 points) The King of Judea bankrolled the Games (which were in financial trouble at the time) and was voted Perpetual President as a result.

4. Hope. (2 points)

5. Socrates again. (2 points) Hemlock is a kind of parsley and belongs to the carrot family. It produces a slow death from paralysis, respiratory failure and stupor.

6. Hafnium. (2 points) The Latin for Copenhagen was Hafnia. Hafnium is the 45th most abundant element in the earth's crust: it's commoner than tin. Hungarian chemist George Charles de Hevesy (1899-1966) and Dutch physicist Dirk Coster (1889-1950) discovered it in Copenhagen in 1923, though neither of them was Danish.

7. Holmium. (2 points) Named after the Latin for Stockholm. Nobody should be expected to know the Latin names for every town in the Roman Empire – *but shouldn't everyone know the names of all the chemical elements?* There are only just over 100 of them…

8. Adrenaline or Epinephrine. (2 points) It is secreted by the triangular adrenal gland that sits on top of the kidneys. In the US, adrenaline is called *epinephrine*. Both words mean 'on' or 'at the kidney': *renes* is Latin for kidneys or loins (French *reins*), *nephros* the Greek. No one knows where the word 'kidney' comes from.

consent, bizarrely, is 12. (No children live there so it's slightly academic, but even so…) It derives from the age of consent in Italy at the time when the Vatican became independent in 1929. The age of consent in Italy is still only 14.

MATHEMATICS, HISTORY, HISTORY OF ART, MODERN LANGUAGES, ARCHAEOLOGY, LINGUISTICS, ENGINEERING, THEOLOGY, ENGLISH & MUSIC

1. Dada. (2 points) The name of the whacky movement, founded by the Romanian Tristran Tzara and patronised by the French poet André Breton, was chosen at random from a French dictionary.

The man who can't visualize a horse galloping on a tomato is an idiot.
ANDRÉ BRETON (1896-1966) *Dadaist and founder of Surrealism*

2. 200. (2 points) A capital H with a line over the top = 200,000.
3. Woodland, or 'Land of Trees'. (2 points)
4a. Honda Civic. (2 points) As a result Honda sold more Japanese cars in America than any other company except Toyota. Soichiro Honda retired the following year.
4b. 'I wish I'd spent more time in the office.' (2 points)
5a. It doesn't mean anything. (2 points) The ice cream was created and named in 1959 and first sold in 1961 by Polish-born New Yorker Reuben Mattus. The name was designed to sound Danish (because of its reputation for dairy products) and the original cartons had a map of Scandinavia on them.
5b. Hungarian. (2 points) To make it even more confusing, the Hungarian for 'Hi!' is 'See ya!' (Szia!)
6. A squishop is a squire who is also a bishop (2 points) **and a squarson is a squire who is also a parson** (2 points). The Hebers were old Yorkshire gentry. Reginald inherited the manor and the living of Hodnet in Shropshire from his father. Like his father, also called Reginald, he became rector there, thus becoming a squarson, and rose to become Bishop of Calcutta hence a squishop.
7. Hiccup. (2 points) This is the accepted spelling today according to the OED. Hiccough is considered an error, in that it's a 'back formation' that comes from a mistaken association with 'cough'. Earlier versions include hickop, hickhop, hicket and hycock, which, like hiccup, are spelt like they sound. In Old English, hiccups (*aelfsogtha*) were thought to be caused by Elves.
(FORFEIT: HICCOUGH. MINUS 2)
8. H or H Minor or H Moll. (Plus 2 points) Appropriately, given that it was his 8th symphony and H is the 8th letter of the alphabet. In the German system of musical nomenclature, the letter H is used for the note (and the scale) of B: the letter B is only used for B flat. B major is called H dur, and B minor is called H moll.
(**MINUS 2 POINTS** for **A, B, C, D, E, F, G** whether sharp, flat, natural, major or minor. **Exceptions are B minor and E major, which would be correct if Schubert had been English: B Minor** scores **0** (1st and 3rd movements), as does **E Major** (2nd movement).

BONUS QUESTION

Cote d'Ivoire. (2 points)
(FORFEIT: IRELAND. MINUS 2 POINTS)

GEOGRAPHY

1. Copenhagen. (2 points) His Grace later had him buried with full military honours and one of his hooves made into an inkwell. A hoof of Marengo, the horse that Napoleon rode at Waterloo is set in silver on the dining room table at the Officer's Mess at St James Palace.
2. One. (2 points) Amsterdam is the only legal city in both Holland and in the Netherlands as a whole. All the others are *gemeente*, 'municipalities'. Dutch law makes no distinction between town and countryside – and if you go there you can see why. This has been the case since 1851, though Napoleon granted a 48-hour charter to The Hague ('The Hedge') in 1811 as he was passing through.
3. The Metropolitan County of Greater Manchester. (2 points) Bolton hasn't been part of the County of Lancashire since 1974.
(FORFEIT: LANCASHIRE. MINUS 2)
4. It's the geographical centre of the British Isles as a whole (the Northern Isles and Channel Islands included). (2 points) Dunsop Bridge, Lancashire, located 71 miles (114 km) south of Haltwhistle, also claims to be the centre of Britain. In 1992, the Ordnance Survey declared Dunsop Bridge the closest village to the centre of Britain, but this was the *gravitational* centre of the *main island* of Britain rather than the *geographical* centre of the British Isles as a whole. The same year, BT marked the occasion by installing its 100,000th payphone on the village green at Dunsop Bridge, complete with a plaque reading 'You are calling from the BT payphone that marks the centre of Britain.' Sir Ranulph Fiennes unveiled the phone box. The precise gravitational centre of Britain is up in the hills 4.3 miles (7 km) outside Dunsop Bridge itself, at Whitendale Hanging Stones, near Brennand Farm. You measure the gravitational centre of a country by cutting out a map and balancing it on a finger. The geographical centre is much more complicated to work out.

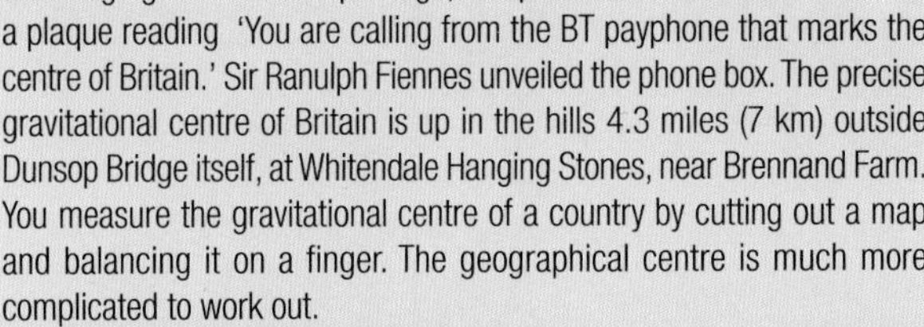

5. Hawaii. (2 points) The 'big island' of Hawaii consists of five volcanoes clumped together. One of them, Mauna Kea, is the tallest mountain in the world measured from base to summit. Its neighbour Mauna Loa ('Long Mountain' in Hawaiian) is the biggest measured by mass: 9,700 cubic miles or 40,000 cu km. From base to summit, Mauna Loa is ¾ mile taller than Everest and, unlike Everest, it stands alone as a distinct mountain, rather than being a high point of a range.
(FORFEIT: HIMALAYAS. MINUS 2)
6. Hispaniola. (2 points) The island is divided between Haiti in the west and the Dominican Republic in the east. About one third is Haiti and two thirds is the Dominican Republic. Columbus claimed the island for Spain in 1492 and named it *La Isla Espanola* ('The Spanish Island').
7. Borshch. (2 points) Any roughly correct spelling will do (plus Russia, Poland, Romania etc.) Borshch was originally made of hogweed. In Russia, the old name for hogweed (*Heracleum sphondylium*) was *borschevnic*. In Poland, both the soup (borshch) and the plant (hogweed) are called *barscz*.
8. The Holy See, aka Vatican City. (2 points) It also has no permanent crops, no arable land, no income tax and no political parties. The age of

Hooray! A handful of Henries!

HENRY KISSINGER (1923-) was christened Heinz.

HENRY HAVELOCK-ELLIS (1859-1939) wrote the first English medical textbook on homosexuality.

Henry, Duke of Cornwall, the first son of HENRY VIII (1491-1547), was born on New Year's Day 1511 and died 52 days later. Had he lived, his father would not have had six wives and England would still be a Catholic country.

SIR HENRY CAMPBELL-BANNERMAN (1836-1908), Britain's first official Prime Minister, was always known as CB but was born plain Henry Campbell.

HENRY COOPER (1934-) is the only boxer to win three Lonsdale belts and was British, European and Commonwealth heavyweight boxing champion.

HENRI DE TOULOUSE LAUTREC (1864-1901) had hypertrophied (enormous) genitals, though it may have just seemed that way because of his very short legs.

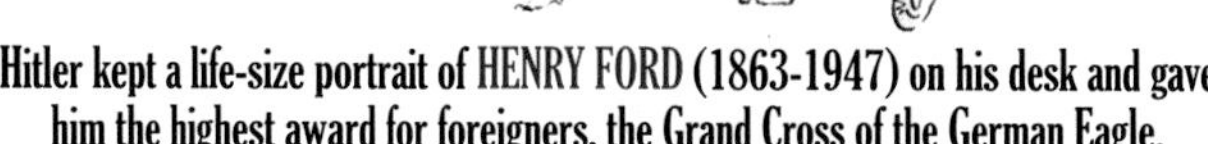

Hitler kept a life-size portrait of HENRY FORD (1863-1947) on his desk and gave him the highest award for foreigners, the Grand Cross of the German Eagle.

HENRY MILLER (1891-1980) once said 'I have no money, no resources, no hopes. I am the happiest man alive.'

HENRY LOUIS 'HL' MENCKEN (1880-1956) was inspired to become a writer on reading 'Huckleberry Finn', aged nine..

HENRY WINKLER (1945-) best known as 'The Fonz', the leather-clad greaser in the TV series 'Happy Days', has never learned to ride a motorcycle.

The family and close friends of HENRY FONDA (1905-82) called him Hank.

OTHER BOOKS FROM QI

The Book of General Ignorance
The Second Book of General Ignorance
The Book of Animal Ignorance
Advanced Banter: The QI Book of Quotations
The QI Book of the Dead
The Sound of General Ignorance
The QI 'E' Annual
The QI 'F' Annual
The QI 'G' Annual

First published in 2010 by Faber and Faber Ltd
Bloomsbury House, 74–77 Great Russell Street, London WC1B 3DA
Printed and bound in Great Britain by Butler Tanner & Dennis, Frome, Somerset

A CIP record for this book is available from the British Library
ISBN 978–0–571–27096–5
2 4 6 8 10 9 7 5 3 1

The QI Annual was researched, written, illustrated, photographed and otherwise enhanced by Glen Baxter, Will Bowen, Jo Brand, Derren Brown, Stevyn Colgan, David Costa, Mat Coward, Cherry Denman, Ted Dewan, Geoff Dunbar, Hunt Emerson, Simon Evans, Arron Ferster, Piers Fletcher, James Harkin, Andy Hollingworth, Tony Husband, Phill Jupitus, Roger Law, Harry Lloyd, John Lloyd, Jim Marks, Brian McFadden, Andy Murray, Nick Newman, Ross Noble, Molly Oldfield, Emmet O'Shea, Aidan Potts, Justin Pollard, Peter Richardson, Brian Ritchie, Morgan Ritchie, Katie Scott, Dan Schreiber, Jen Sorensen, Adrian Teal, Robert Thompson, Johnny Vegas and Guy Venables.

The QI Annual features Stephen Fry, Alan Davies and the guest panellists from the QI TV 'H' series: Chris Addison, Ronni Ancona, Bill Bailey, Danny Baker, Clare Balding, Jo Brand, Gyles Brandreth, Rob Brydon, Jimmy Carr, Jeremy Clarkson, Jack Dee, Rich Hall, Andy Hamilton, Eddie Izzard, Phill Jupitus, John Lloyd, Sean Lock, Fred MacAulay, Lee Mack, David Mitchell, Ross Noble, Graham Norton, Dara O'Briain, Sue Perkins, Daniel Radcliffe, Sandi Toksvig, Johnny Vegas, Ruby Wax and Robert Webb.

Designed by David Costa (Wherefore Art?) Email david@whereforeart.com
Cover illustration: Peter Richardson: nina@illustrationweb.com

Editorial: Sarah Lloyd
Editorial Administrator: Liz Townsend

Picture Research: Liz Townsend with David Costa and John Lloyd

Photography:
Andy Hollingworth (andyhollingworth@me.com) for 'Home Economy' and 'The Happy Potter'; Jim Marks (www.marks.co.uk) for 'Five Holiday at Home'; and Brian Ritchie (brian@brianjritchie.com) for the QI production photographs and 'Haka'

The QI researchers and writers for *The QI Annual* were: Will Bowen, Mat Coward, Arron Ferster, Piers Fletcher, James Harkin, John Lloyd, John Mitchinson, Andy Murray, Molly Oldfield, Justin Pollard and Dan Schreiber.

QI Logo design: Jules Bailey

With special thanks to Henry Worsley; Claire Nightingale; Derren Brown; Harpy, Phil and Grove Rugby Club (www.groverfc.co.uk): Lisa Hammond, founder of Adopt a Potter Charity, for the use of Maze Hill Pottery studio, assisted by Darren and Brigitte; Nick Goff and staff, North Somerset Museum, Weston-super-Mare (www.n-somerset.gov.uk/museum); Dinah Howland for her painting of Gordon the Greyhound in 'Halo!'; Mick Pedroli and David Milne at Dennis Severs House, and Harry Lloyd and Jack Prendergast for their assistance on 'Home Economy'; Script to Screen (www.scripttoscreen.co.uk) for the Victorian bathing costumes in 'Holiday at Home' and to Dudley the donkey for his appearance in same.

Photo credits: Alamy for Dunsop Bridge in 'H Quiz'; Bigstockphoto (www.bigstockphoto.com) for saint praying and St David in 'Halo!' and background pictures in 'Horology', except Faceless Clock which was photographed by John Cory Fenton (www.fentonphotographer.com); Mary Evans Picture Library (www.maryevans.com) for Franz Schubert and Wellington in 'H Quiz Answers'; Bridgeman Art Library (www.bridgemanart.com) for St Bruno, Martyrdom of St Denis and Saint Valerie in 'Halo!', and William Blake's 'The Ancient of Days' in 'Health & Safety'; Corbis Images (www.corbisimages.com) for Golda Meir, Karl Marx, Ron Jeremy, Gene Simmons and Albert Einstein in 'Hirsute Hebrews'; Getty Images for Groucho Marx, Mark Spitz and Samson in 'Hirsute Hebrews', and Moon Plaque, Alexander the Great and Hummingbird in 'H Quiz Answers' ; St Eulalia in 'Halo!' © Tate, London 2010; AAA Ancient Art & Architecture Collection for Neptune in 'Halo!', Afghan rug in 'Helmand' photographed by Kevin Sudeith, courtesy of warrug.com; Shutterstock Images (www.shutterstock.com) for photographs in 'Hot or Not?', also St Colman in 'Halo!' and Haredi Jew in 'Hirsute Hebrews'; Photograph of Stephen Fry by Mark Harrison for *Radio Times*.

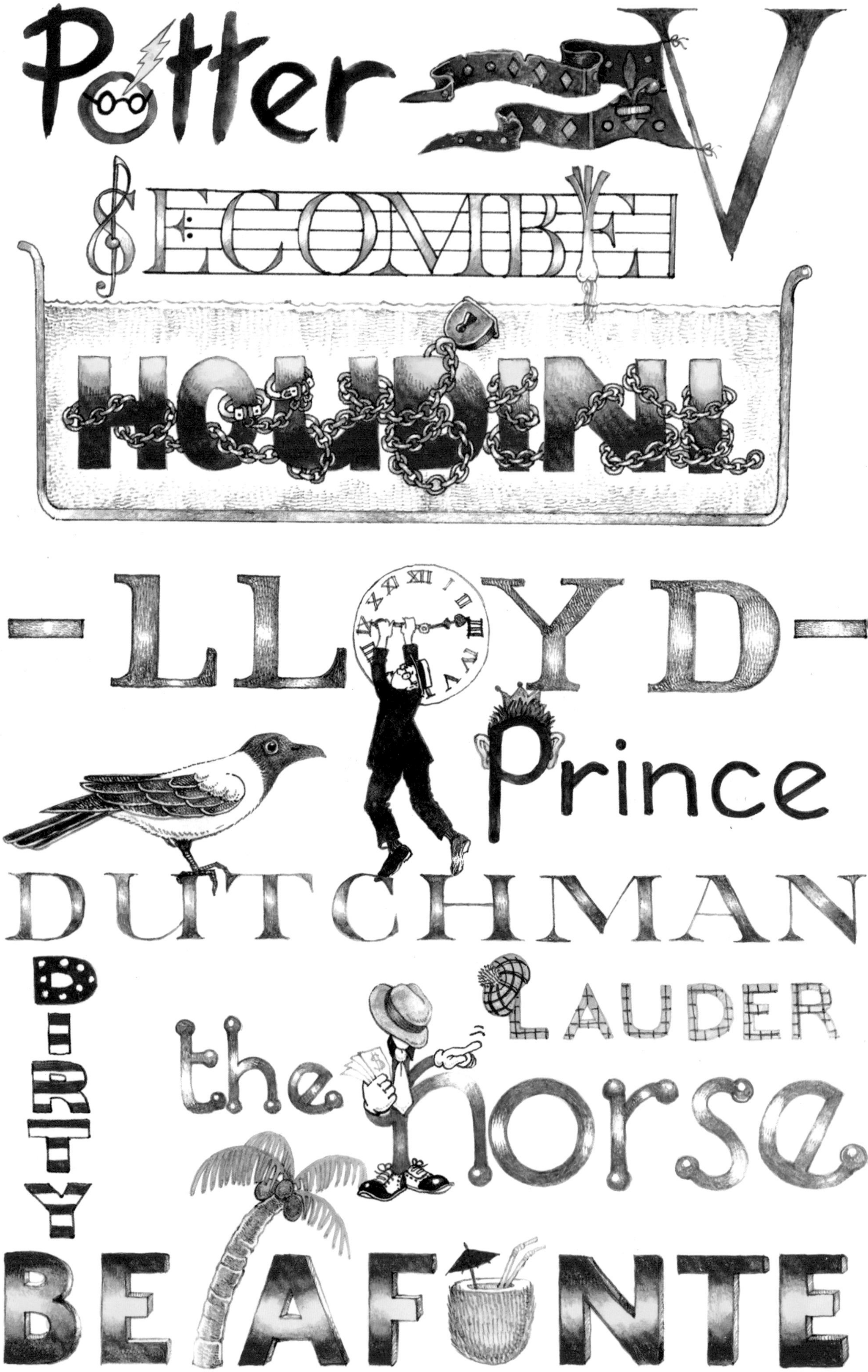

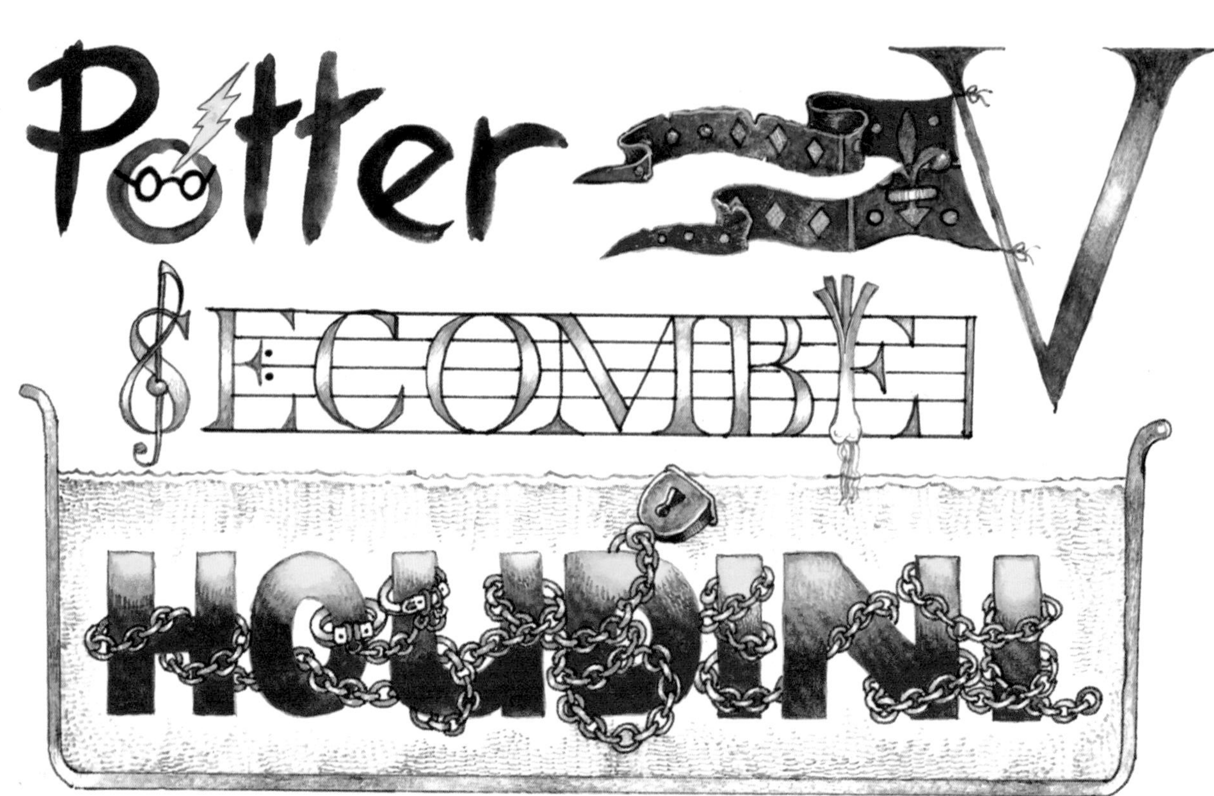

Potter
V
SECOMBE
HOUDINI
LLOYD
Prince
DUTCHMAN
DIRTY
LAUDER
the horse
BELAFONTE